The Writers' Mill Journal

Volume 6

2017

ISBN-13: 978-1974506460

ISBN-10: 1974506460

First printed by Createspace, October 2017

COMPILED BY

Judy Beaston, Sheila Deeth, and Jean Harkin

EDITED BY

Carolyn Adams, Richard David Bach, Judy Beaston,
Sheila Deeth, Jean Harkin, Karin Krafft, Robin Layne,
Joe and Carol Ann Mendez, and Zaferia Russell

COVER PHOTOGRAPH BY

Karen Alexander-Brown

INTERIOR DESIGN BY

Judy Beaston, Sheila Deeth, and Jean Harkin

ILLUSTRATED BY

Carolyn Adams, Karen Alexander-Brown,
Susan Apurado, Judy Beaston, Sheila Deeth, Steven Deeth,
Amelia De Mello, Jean Harkin, Micah Harkin, Robin Layne,
Kelly Passalaqua, and Louise Young.

PICTURE EDITING BY

Sheila Deeth

With thanks to Ron Davis and Pati Burraston for generously sharing
their technical and artistic know-how.

DEDICATED to all the talented, creative and hard-working writers, editors and illustrators who made this journal happen, and the members of The Writers' Mill writing group who so generously support, critique and encourage each other in their writing endeavors.

THANKS also to the Cedar Mill Community Library staff for their continuing support of our writers' group.

CONTRIBUTORS

Carolyn Adams' poetry, photography, and collage art have been published in *Forge*, *Rockhurst Review*, and *Caveat Lector*, among others. She has authored four chapbooks with the most recent being *The Things You've Left Behind*. Recently relocated from Houston, Texas, she now lives in Beaverton, Oregon.

David Lutes enjoys writing short stories from an international perspective. He lived twenty years in Japan, Hong Kong and Malaysia. He looks forward to finishing his first novel this winter in Mexico.

Jean Harkin is a regular contributor to *The Writers' Mill Journal*. Her first novel was selected as a finalist in the Maple Lane Books 2016 publishing contest. Her book of short stories, *Night in Alcatraz: And Other Uncanny Tales* is now available online. Jean can be found online at www.goodreads.com/jeanatwritersmill

Jessie Collins lives in England. She is Sheila Deeth's mother, and she enjoys joining the Writers' Mill each year when she visits her daughter in Oregon.

Joe Mendez has been writing since the 1990s and has one article published in *Guideposts Magazine* in their December 1995 issue. He is working on his eighth novel. He will publish his first three novels in the next several months.

Judy Beaston finds inspiration for her writing from the people and natural beauty of the Pacific Northwest. Her poems and stories have appeared at *Three Line Poetry*, *Poetry Quarterly*, *Indiana Voice Journal*, *Writers' Mill Journal Volume 3,4&5*, *Writer's Type,* and in an anthology of short stories titled *The Way Back*. She has been a member of Writers' Mill since 2009.

Karen Alexander-Brown first honed her authorial skills by writing as a pastime while on tours as a professional dancer. She's the author and producer of several short plays and a musical for the Fertile Ground Festival, has written several published academic articles, and currently writes fiction, creative non-fiction and memoir.

Karin Krafft has enjoyed writing most of her life, but not seriously until five years ago when she joined a writing group on a NATO Base in Belgium. She tries to write a short story a month and has co-authored a thriller called *The Cruise* by Jake Corey and Joy Christian. (Joy Christian is the name Karin used while writing the novel, in case it was a total flop! The e-book is available online.)

Lauri Leonetti, a native Oregonian and remedial reading specialist, ventured into hobby writing in 2004 with an online writing course and a writing conference, after which she tumbled into participating in NaNoWriMo (National Novel Writing Month—a challenge she's enjoyed for several years), but she's new at sharing her work. She appreciates the Writers' Mill for the incentive to do so, and to branch into other composition forms.

Mary Jane Erickson began photography and writing stories and poems to accompany her piano lessons at the age of eleven. Currently, her writings have been published in various journals, with photography displayed at professional showings, including the Oregon State Fair.

Matthew McAyeal writes mainly historical fiction, fantasy, and comedy. In 2008, two screenplays he wrote were semi-finalists in the Screenplay Festival.

Richard David Bach is a recovering lawyer writing in Lake Oswego. He has published the four volume Common Denominator Series of romantic thrillers (*Common Enemy*, *Common Ground*, *Common Place* and *Common Sense*) and is working on a fifth in the series (tentatively titled *Common Cause*). Richard is a new member of Writer' Mill, and is pleased to have joined.

Robin Layne has published a number of poems and won some short story contests. She does freelance editing while working on a series of YA vampire novels and writing stories and poems using prompts from writers' groups.

Sheila Deeth is the author of the *Five-Minute Bible Story Series*™ published by Cape Arago Press, *Tails of Mystery*, published by Linkville Press, and *the Mathemafiction Novels*, published by Indigo Sea Press Find her at sheiladeeth.com.

Susan Apurado RN "came into this world to bring a glorious Sunshine to the clouded spirits. To spring radiance and beauty to the hearts of those away from the limelight." A wife, mother and nurse, avid photographer and fine arts painter for whom poetry is her daily dose, she joined the Writers' Mill after moving from the Philippines to the US. Her work has been published in college newspapers and the *International Library Of Poetry Anthology*.

Zaferia Russell has lived in Oregon for 27 years. She has been a lifelong writer, starting with her journals in elementary school, leading to her humorist observation pieces of today. Presently, she is working on two novels—a young adult fictional piece and a book about the lifelong relationship of two women who have seen it all, done it all and lived to tell the tale!

CONTENTS

Writers' Mill Contest Winners
included in this journal

1st place August 2016 Photo Inspired: The Duprass by Robin Layne

2nd place August 2016 Photo Inspired: The Pact by Karen Alexander-Brown

3rd place August 2016 Photo Inspired: Empty Heart by Judy Beaston

1st place September 2016 Last Time I Saw…: The Architect by Karin Krafft

1st place September 2016 Last Time I Saw…: Flowers by Sheila Deeth

2nd place September 2016 Last Time I Saw…: Teddy by Lauri Leonetti

3rd place September 2016 Last Time I Saw…: As in Identical by Robin Layne

1st place December 2016 Ring: Halo in the Dark by Karen Alexander-Brown

2nd place December 2016 Ring: Unmentionable Term by Lauri Leonetti

1st place January 2017 Be Inspired: Refuge by Karen Alexander-Brown

3rd place January 2017 Be Inspired: Dark and Stormy Knight by Robin Layne

1st place March 2017 Full Moon: Cat on the Moon by Jean Harkin

3rd place March 2017 Full Moon: The Wolves by Matthew McAyeal

2nd place April 2017 Wonder: Wonder by Jessie Collins

1st place May 2017 Unspoken Bonds: Across the Wall by Matthew McAyeal

2nd place May 2017 Unspoken Bonds: Talk too Much by Sheila Deeth

3rd place May 2017 Unspoken Bonds: Points of View by Jean Harkin

3rd place May 2017 Unspoken Bonds: Secret Lives by Robin Layne

1st place June 2017 Water Water…: Mirage by Karen Alexander-Brown

2nd place June 2017 Water Water…: Undercurrent by Jean Harkin

3rd place June 2017 Water Water…: Splashes of Childhood by Judy Beaston

1st place July 2017 For Art's Sake: Art For Art's Sake by Richard David Bach

2nd place July 2017 For Art's Sake: Lisa's Portrait by Judy Beaston

3rd place July 2017 For Art's Sake: Slave by Robin Layne

MEMORIES

Minnie and Roseanna from the Writers' Mill group photograph 2015
photographed by Amelia De Mello

WHERE by Sheila Deeth
in memory of JeanAnn, Roseanna, Minnie, Jack
and all Writers' Millers gone before us

Where do unfinished stories go—
Lives with pages yet unwrit
Tales of wonder, joy and wit
And mysteries yet unknown?

Where now are the unicorns
You poured upon the printed page
To prance on your imagined stage?
They've lost their shape and form.

Where now is the mystery
And who will tell the story's end
Or will another one befriend
Your muse and start again?

Where do unfinished stories go?
They wait upon the passing breeze.
They float upon the wafting seas.
They wave to be set free, if we'd but know.

And you, my friends
Who go before
Know only now beginnings
Never ends.

REMEMBERING ROSEANNA by Robin Layne

I met Roseanna Ellis in spring 2008 in a Write Around Portland group at its office in Portland. The group, Write On, was for people who had completed two Write Around Portland workshops in the Portland area. Write Around Portland facilitators lead these workshops for people who usually don't get a voice, and they write in community to short, timed prompts. Write On created broadsides—posters featuring our writings. For our group, Roseanna wrote a beautiful nature poem called "Spring Painting." We mostly remember Roseanna's preoccupation with what she *didn't* have— her amputated foot—but this poem was happy and mentioned nothing about amputation.

Roseanna was devastated by the loss of her foot. It happened because she was outside and got frostbite that developed gangrene. She fiercely blamed herself for the neglect and identified herself with misery and stigma. I was haunted by one of the poems she wrote in which she called herself "devil's food." Someone said the poem wasn't true. But it was Roseanna's emotional reality at the time, however warped it might have seemed to people on the outside.

That summer we shared the advanced class, Seasoned Writers, which we all took turns facilitating. We learned about zines (usually do-it-yourself booklets), and we created our own, called *Repeat Offenders*, with two pages devoted to each writer. Roseanna included two "Sonnets to My Foot" and a short poem about Amputee Island. Her poetry contrasted the frustrations of disability with a sense of freedom and joy and a love of the beauty around her.

I ran into Roseanna at a later date. She proudly gave me a plain white copy of her book, *Amputee Island*, which she had printed at Powell's City of Books.

I was pleased to meet up with her yet again, here in the Writers' Mill. She was a member for a long time—possibly since the group's onset in October 2007. One of her contributions to our *Zeus and Bo and Fred and Joe and Co* collection features a dog and cat so free they fly back and forth from the moon to the earth. The earth-bound dog and cat they meet, though themselves unable to fly, are swept up in the joy of their company.

I hope Roseanna is now freer than she ever was even before her injury—running barefoot, as she longed to do, and flying like Moondoggy.

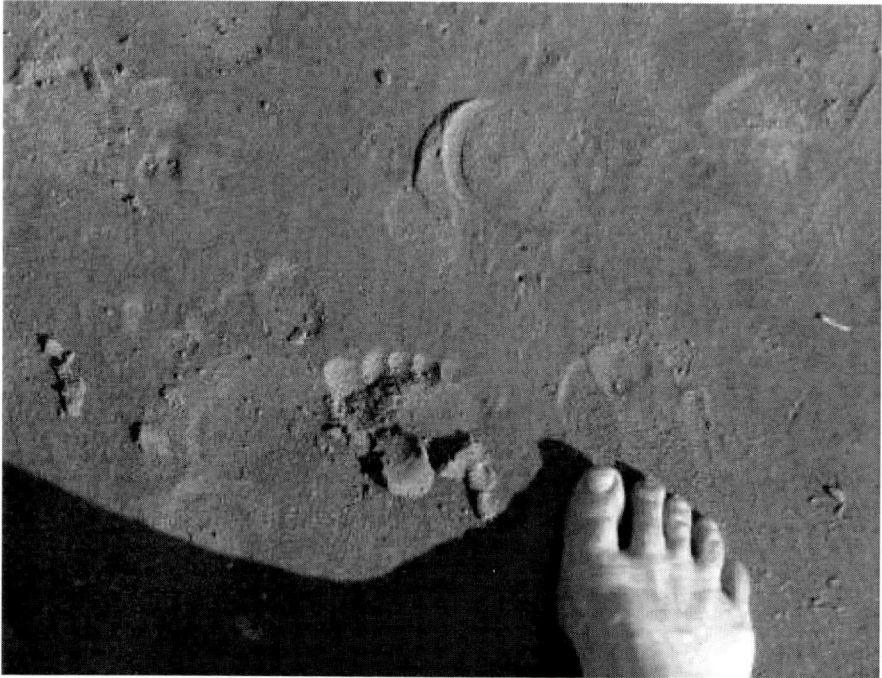

Footprints photographed by Carolyn Adams

IN SILENCE by Susan Apurado
in memory of my sister Joy, 1967-2017

I smiled too often to hide the pain
But in silence
My swollen heart is soaked in rain

I walked off from the deepest sorrow
But in silence
The distance I bridged is hard to follow

I pretended to be always reasonably well
But in silence
Grieving has stages to surely dwell

I held back my fears and tears
But in silence
It appears, thinking all those years

Alas! Like a radiant rose in early summer
Withered in silence
I was left in disgust; to God, I surrender…

Photograph by Susan Apurado

5

FOR MINNIE by Mary Jane Erickson

You have shared your life
With your faith in God
Bringing this love to your family
And those in the world
To bring spiritual healing and peace to others
In God's created universe.
Now you are home
In the peace of the heavens.
Your loving message will live on
Through the written words
You have joyfully given
And will always continue
In this life, and the future.

Minnie's Minnie Bible: one of many at the "free items table" at her memorial service where she continued giving Christian literature beyond her earthly life. She marked verses that lead the reader to salvation and the expectation of Christ's return.

Photo by Kelly Passalaqua, planned and modeled by Robin Layne

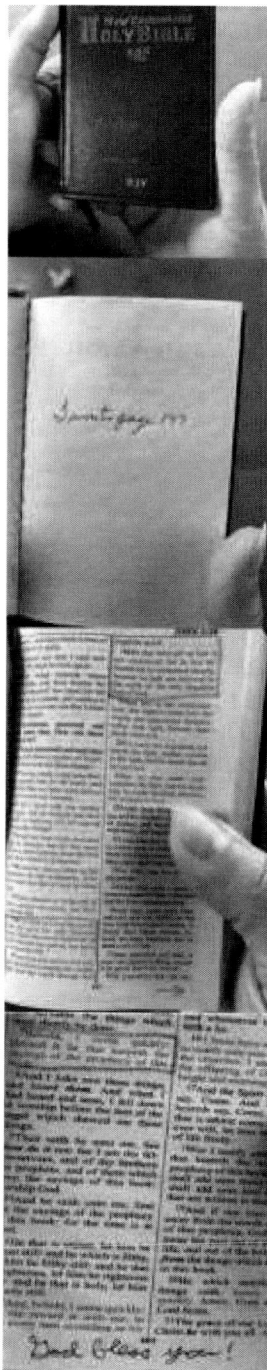

MIGHTY MINNIE IS MISSED... BUT NOT LOST
by Robin Layne

I met Minnie Stoumbaugh the first time she showed up at the writers' critique group that used to meet at the Beaverton Library. She brought a manuscript about her work for Wycliffe Bible translators—an organization I'd dreamed of working for when I was younger, a dream that never came true for me. It was both surprising and exciting to learn that this little elderly lady, who was so petite she brought a decorated cardboard box to meetings to use as a footstool, had joined this ministry at age fifty (just a few years younger than I am!), travelled all around the world, and had even been in the service as a Marine. A *Marine!* Makes you think *anything* is possible!

She invited me to the Writers' Mill, a much larger group that still meets at the Cedar Mill Library. I started going to that, and I continue to be an active member. The writers in that group are very practiced and talented, and we are proud to have had Minnie among our numbers. Some of her short and humorous memories were published in Volume 5 of *The Writers' Mill Journal*. We hope Minnie's memoir of her adventures with Wycliffe can be completed posthumously and published. Some of us are willing to help.

Some stories I remember from her Wycliffe memoir: In a camp trying out new candidates to Wycliffe, Minnie showed off the one muscle in her arm and told the others to remember her as "Mighty Minnie from Mining, Idaho." *I* for one won't forget Mighty Minnie!

She learned that during coffee breaks on the mission field, newcomers could be recognized by their complaints about the ants in the sugar. Missionaries who had been working for maybe a year would calmly scoop out the ants with a spoon. But old-timers would look at the sugar and demand, "Where are the ants?"

Minnie was always kind, gave me a lot of rides home from the Writers' Mill meetings and sometimes to my church. In the small critique group, which I took over when the librarian who facilitated it retired, Minnie helped me as she could with my current writing project, even though she made it plain that the subject matter, and fiction in general, was not her cup of tea. Not long ago, she left my critique group because of this distaste and her feeling that she wasn't able to help with my novel. Nevertheless, in the last email I received from her she sent information about that subject matter and encouraged me in the project—an act that showed the largeness of her dear heart.

Minnie was ready to take another trip, and was frustrated by car trouble. Perhaps that car trouble was the hand of God, to keep her at home just a little longer, before He took her much farther away—into the adventure of eternity.

We will always remember her spitfire energy, which never left her to the unexpected end of her life among us. But I cannot talk of Minnie in the past tense. I know she can never die and that I will see her again in Heaven.

Minnie's Mighty Muscle by Robin Layne

ART, MUSIC AND MORE

Pastoral, painting by Karen Alexander-Brown

LISA'S PORTRAIT by Judy Beaston

There's a little fleck of paint on the tip of Leo's nose. Perhaps if I stare at that, I shall relax more into the soft smile he demands. Unless my thoughts drift to the silly ways his tongue peeks out ever-so-slightly between those dark lips. Dark lips and serious eyes. This man cannot be any woman's first catch of the evening. But how might I make him lighten up just a bit? I do need a break. His intensity is like sun blazing down on me in the courtyard on those days I want to keep my distance from Francesco.

I'm meant to be serious about posing for this portrait, but what comes to mind is a satire of my life. He places me before a scene reminiscent of nothing I am allowed. Oh, to escape up that road, find solace in the mountains, be anywhere but here.

I've been told a half-smile is the most relaxed position for the face. Not for me. I shall be lucky if I can even move my mouth after this session. And my feet are falling asleep. As are my hands stuck on these arm rests built for a giant of a man and not my own stature.

Truly this is the most boring task I've ever undertaken. If he'd paint faster and stop being such a perfectionist, we'd be done by now. I need to visit the market for sausages, tomatoes and onions on the way home today. And some peppermint. My mouth is terribly dry from sitting here with this pasted-on smile. But will we be done before the market closes? What will Francesco say if I do not make his Tagliatelle tonight?

Francesco. If you had not caught Leo in bed with Marcella, he would not owe you this portrait and I would be free to work on my needlepoint and music, walk in the woods behind our house or stroll along the quay with my mother and sister.

Too many days of long hours drives spikes of pain along my spine. But, Leo has promised an end to this madness only when it suits him. I wonder… perhaps if I found his soft center beneath those worn clothes, his work might be inspired toward its completion?

Ah, there, he steps back. A good sign? No, no, no. He is shaking his head, looking to the floor. Leo, Leo, Leo—you must end this madness!

"I am finished." He sits upon a stool near his work bench. "You are done."

"The painting is completed? I may leave?" My body is unresponsive. Stiff. First the smile must go. Let him stare or laugh, I must open my mouth wide, move my jaw. Turn my head. Next my hands and arms, struggling with pins and needles as nerves reawaken.

"No," he speaks at last. "I cannot be engaged with this mistake any longer."

I freeze in place. What does this mean? I shift my body, stare at his shadowed eyes, slackened jaw, shocked that this man could ever give up on anything.

"Wait!" He jumps up, grabs his palette. "Don't move. That expression. Perfect!"

At last, he paints with enthusiastic brush strokes. The entire room vibrates with heightened energy. I dare not breathe, though I must. Shallow breaths as if enduring a tiring moment at the hands of Francesco.

Seconds hammer away in the old clock on his mantle. Each note a reminder of the meal I will not prepare tonight. Even if the market vendors remain, the best food shall be gone. But I don't mind. I am mesmerized by Leo's artistry in motion.

A smile draws wide upon his face. "Yes!"

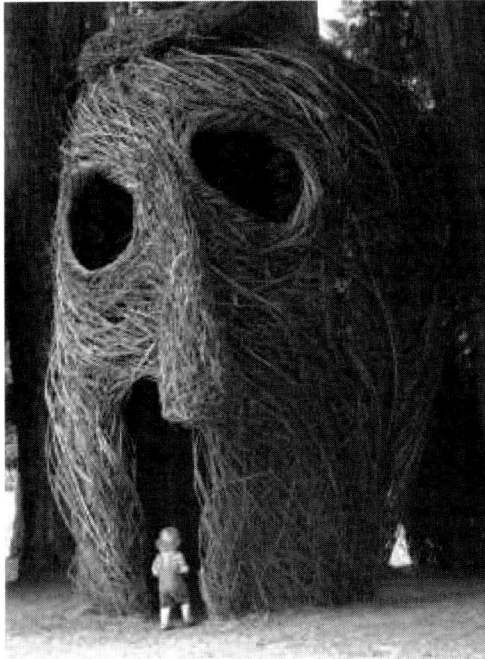

"Head over Heels" willow and dogwood branch sculpture by Patrick Dougherty, Orenco Woods Nature Park, Hillsboro, Oregon. Photographed by Jean Harkin, used with permission.

SOMETHING GOOD WORTH LIVIN' by Susan Apurado

Geese flipping, geese flopping
Hissing, whistling breezes
Hinking and honking
Skein, on my eyesight, pleases
Across the glass window
In my solitary moment
It draws a smile, and greatly appeases
To the souls gently releases
A cup of ill emotion and reinvent…

How lovely is the day
To feel the warm beds of nature
And hear a song of a lovely creature
Dancing in the sky of delight
Even if your heart is belted with sorrows
Even if your mind is clouded with fears
Keep the sunlight within
For in this life we borrowed
There's always something good worth livin'…

Something Good photographed by Susan Apurado

ME AND MY SHADOW by Robin Layne
A tribute to Robin Williams, and to the child in all of us
(Song lyrics)

I went to see a movie 'bout a little man who flew,
And when he went to Neverland, he took me with him, too.
Like him I remembered things that I'd forgot I knew.
Me and my shadow got some catching up to do.

I caught her in the parking lot, we splashed in all the water,
I chased her through a field of grass and gardens with my daughter.
I don't know where she's been but now I'm glad today I got her,
I found you, shadow, and I'm catching up to you.

(chorus:)
If you're without a shadow, you're a clock that doesn't run.
I knew I was just marking time 'til I got back my fun.

I talked into the night with my flying man, the Shadow Maker,
He brought back all my dreams He resurrected from the breaker.
He told me that the past is past, don't be a bellyacher;
I found you, shadow, and I'm catching up to you.

(chorus:)
If you're without a shadow, you're a clock that doesn't run.
I knew I was just marking time 'til I got back my fun.

I'm glad that I'm a mommy, that's the happy thought I found.
My heart is in the heavens though my feet stay on the ground.
The place where we're all children's where I live and where I'm bound.
Dance with me, shadow…

Cast by the Light of the World.

Song written soon after the movie Hook *came out, and recorded on the CD* Faithful, *released in July 2016. Lyrics published in* Enlarging the Tent: Poetry and Prose by Robin Layne, *2000 and 2011;* Sweet Comfort *newsletter (March 2007); and* NAMI News *January 2017.*

KITKIT'S PICTURE BOX by Sheila Deeth

Kitkit's people lived in a world of boxes. Their home was like a box, with windows letting in the light and doors allowing entry to people, pets and *things*. Inside the house, each room was a box with its own windows and doors. Each box was furnished with snuggly soft boxes to sit and lie on, and solid boxes on which the people stood things. Frequently there were boxes stacked on boxes. A box was sometimes left in the water-room, filled with pellets from another box and suitably arranged for the needs of well-mannered cats. Other boxes held lights and sound and slipped out of pockets and folds in people's extra skins. But Kitkit did not carry any boxes in her fur. Kitkit wasn't a people; she was a cat.

People often went out in their box on wheels, called a car, and returned carrying box-shaped bags all filled with boxes of food. These treasures were stored behind doors in big boxes in the kitchen. At appropriate times of day, food was tipped from smaller boxes into the cats' and dogs' dishes. Sometimes food was put on plates for Kitkit's people too. Often their food didn't come out of boxes but was rich and brightly colored with things that grow in the ground. Sometimes the smell of people-food made Kitkit purr like a lion.

When Kitkit was small, she learned lots of interesting things about people-food from Fred and Joe, the dogs who lived in her house. Kitkit learned to sneak into the kitchen and open the door-box called a cupboard under the water-box called a sink. A left-overs-box called a waste bin contained delicious bites that entertained and fed the dogs and cats every night, over and again—as long as nobody caught them.

Then there was the big flat box in the living room. This box was usually black but sometimes brightly colored. It contained lots of noise which exploded out with the colors. If Kitkit tried very hard, sat very still, and listened very intently, she could sometimes believe she was seeing and hearing more people and more boxes inside the big black box. But she could never find them, no matter how hard she tried.

Sometimes Kitkit saw cats and lions inside the big black box. Sometimes they roared.

Kitkit's people seemed to see and hear many interesting things from this box. They often sat on soft boxes to stare at it, absorbed for hours on end.

One day the man brought another flat box into the house from the four-wheeled car-box. This was a box wrapped in thick brown stuff and tied with string. Kitkit sniffed eagerly, hoping the box might contain cats and lions. But all she smelled was paper and shopping things.

The man and woman removed the covering from the box. Inside was a flat brown rectangle containing a splash of multiple colors and shapes. The colors didn't make any noise. Kitkit thought perhaps they were broken, and wondered why the people didn't switch them off. They always switched off the colors on the big black box when the noises stopped.

Instead the man and woman lifted the rectangle up against a wall. The man made lots of banging sounds, the woman muttered and moaned—"This way. No that"—the baby gurgled and wrapped itself in reams of brown paper and string, and finally the flat brown box was attached to the wall. It must have still been switched on, since the colors didn't go away. But Kitkit was still very puzzled as it continued to make no sound.

Kitkit tried sitting very still, listening very intently, tipping her head and her ears on one side and then the other, and twitching her whiskers and eyes. Gradually she made the colors of the new box come together. Slowly she worked out what they were. And then she felt a gurgling purr in her throat, like a lion's quiet growl, while her tail began to twitch and her whiskers to prick, and the purr grew furiously loud. *Not right! Not right!*

The big brown box contained a picture—very still and silent—of *dogs*! It was a picture of dogs, sitting on chair-boxes, set around a big flat table-box, playing with flat things that might have been phone-boxes except they were white rather than black. The flat things had red and black shapes on them—hearts, diamonds, clover-leaves, and something a bit like trees. The dogs had drinks in glass boxes near their paws and were dressed in people-skins. It was all very odd. And nothing moved or spoke.

Kitkit arched her back as she stared at the picture. *Dogs! Why did it have to be dogs?* Then she trotted down the corridor to the box that was the little child's room. Inside the room she found the box where people-toys were kept. Inside the box she found a box where flat pieces of card were kept. And inside the box filled with flat pieces of card, she found white cards with red and black spots, just like in the picture on the wall!

Kitkit carried these cards gently in her mouth, one by one, into the living room. She laid them out on the carpet in front of the window that was sometimes a door. She tugged her water-bowl from the kitchen, setting it next to one of the fanned out sets of cards. Then she tugged some people-skins from the basket in the water-room. Finally she sat down beside her mother, beside the cards.

Cats can play at this game too, Kitkit thought.

It wasn't clear what the human woman thought, but she ran to her bedroom-box and came out with a thin black phone-box. It flashed a red light and clicked a few times, after which the woman told the man and the child to come and look. Kitkit came too, though the picture was very small and hard to see. She had to sit very still, listen very intently, tip her head and her ears on one side and then the other, and twitch her whiskers and eyes. Then the shapes on the phone-box screen changed from liquid dark into light, making a picture, just like the picture on the wall. Except this one was of Kitkit and Cat wearing people-clothes and playing with people-cards—a much better image, though small.

The man said *"Poker Game* for cats." The child said "Ugh." And the woman pushed buttons on her little black phone-box, making the big black picture-box wake into noise and life. She pushed more buttons to stop the noise, then laughed and said, "That's right." But what was right?

Kitkit sat very still, listened very intently, tipped her head and twitched her whiskers and eyes; and then she saw it—a picture on the big black picture-box machine. It was a picture just like the dog-picture on the wall, but this was a Cat and Kitkit picture: Cat and Kitkit with water-bowl and cards. This was a much better image, Kitkit thought. So she lay down and fell asleep staring at the wondrous, though oddly silent, picture-box, while her tiny tail twitched and her tiny throat purred and purred and purred.

Purrington's Cat photographed by Jean Harkin

SLAVE by Robin Layne

Light laughter breaks upon the lips,
Covers up the pain,
Years of longing, ages of unrest
Gone by
But never lost.
Strong hands yield more years of bondage and fear,
Young body grows old reaping food for another,
Emotion the rich man will never know.
The clank of chains is just beyond hearing,
A free spirit screams with the lash of a whip.
Only the spirit is broken
Every day.

Shall I be comforted with what I have?
I'd rather be friends with the darkness
For none is more a slave than he
In the chains of a numb heart
Vacant of feeling,
Of knowing,
Of understanding.
I hear the screams and shrink in sorrow,
I know the pain and soak in tears.
Comfort me not
For I would rather be free
To know, to feel, to hurt,
To be the slave
So I may learn to love.

Fetters by Robin Layne

Written in reaction to the mini-series Roots. *Published in* The Phoenix, *El Modena High School, 1977 and* Enlarging the Tent: Poetry and Prose by Robin Layne*, 2000 and 2011.*

NIGHTHAWKS by Karin Krafft

"Your assignment today is to describe Edward Hopper's painting 'Nighthawks' in less than five hundred words. You have thirty minutes and then we'll have a discussion." The voice belongs to someone who I assume is the professor.

"Edward Hopper who?" the skinny blonde sitting next to me whispers, looking like a living question mark. She looks too young to be in college.

Before I have time to answer, the professor puts up the painting on the large screen.

"I assume you've all seen this painting by Edward Hopper before?" says the voice with the thick rimmed glasses.

Describe a painting? Am I in the wrong class? A quick check, however, reveals that I am where I am supposed to be. Composition 102. Supposed to be an easy class and easy credit. I have no clue about art. Besides, I have no interest in art, none whatsoever.

What's with the professor's voice? Can he sound any more boring? Sure, I've seen this painting before, but I hadn't been impressed then, and I'm still not impressed. Not much to tell really. Three people in a diner in some city. A couple and a single man. And a cook. Obviously, it is late at night, the streets are empty and the streetlights are on. And what does this have to do with English composition? People around me are writing furiously already. What could there be to write about?

I look at the screen again. Maybe the couple are having an affair? They're sure taking a big chance eating together at a diner in the middle of a city. Except maybe one of them isn't from there and they only meet occasionally. Definitely having an affair. Married couples don't go to diners in the middle of the night, do they?

"Focus." The professor interrupts my thoughts. "What do you think the artist is trying to convey?"

The professor's voice is driving me crazy. He seriously sounds like a recording and what's with all the questions. *What is the artist trying to convey? Hello, this is an English class, not an arts class.* I bet Mr. Thick Rimmed Boring has never been to a diner late at night, and especially not with a beautiful woman. He probably wants to know what it feels like to have a life. *Okay, now you're being mean, you don't know anything about this guy. Concentrate on the assignment.*

Wait a minute. That guy with the redhead looks like Uncle George. Uncle George always wears a blue suit and a hat. But why is he wearing a hat inside? But that gorgeous redhead is not Auntie Liz. And doesn't Ms. Gorgeous Redhead know that redheads aren't supposed to wear red? What is she doing with Uncle George? Is she having an affair with Uncle George? How could he do that do Auntie Liz? She is such a nice lady. Did she know? And why did she stay with him? I remembered the whispers at family dinners about Uncle George being a real charmer. It hadn't sounded like a compliment.

"Having a hard time with this one?"

The boring professor is obviously referring to my blank sheet of paper. Blank except for my name written neatly in the top left-hand corner.

"It doesn't matter if you don't know the painting." The professor drones on.

Go away. How can I concentrate with you hovering over me? I desperately want to scream this out loud, but I do have manners after all. As he moves on, the scent trailing him just about knocks me out. He's seriously overdosed with the cologne. Who is he trying to impress? Obviously not his wife; no wedding ring. But maybe he is one of those guys who never wears his wedding ring. He could have an allergy, or maybe he is a cheater too, like Uncle George and that's why he chose this painting. Or maybe he just needs to hide his personality, or lack thereof.

"Okay people, focus. Ten more minutes."

The blonde next to me who had never heard of Edward Hopper has filled two pages and is starting on page three. Hadn't she heard him say less than five hundred words? At least I had less than that. So, I was following the instructions. And she was not.

The woman in the painting is quite intriguing. Is that the kind of woman Uncle George likes? Auntie Liz is a brunette, well now she is more gray, but this is an old painting. The woman doesn't even seem interested in Uncle George. Come to think of it, he doesn't seem very interested in her either. Uncle George looks very uncomfortable. Has the cook recognized him? It looks like they are having a discussion. Is he feeling guilty? Poor Auntie Liz. And what about the other guy? Is that curvy redhead flirting with him? It's hard to see from the picture. Is she cheating on Uncle George already?

Okay, stop. It's not really Uncle George.

"Okay class, time over. Who wants to read what they have written?"

Not me obviously. I look around at my fellow students and they all seem to have at least two pages and seem eager to share their brilliance.

My paper is still blank, except for my name and one added sentence. *Scene from a diner.* So much for an easy class and easy credit. No problem, easy to make up later.

But I am so disappointed in Uncle George.

Diner Window in Winter photographed by Sheila Deeth

LIFE CHANGES by Susan Apurado

Painting by Susan Apurado

Beauty of wonders yonder
In the stillness of the forest.
As this soul's eyes wander
And ponder on the galaxy of stars.
When the tide of time changes,
I sail myself across the river of life
To the enormous current,
Right where I need it to be.

Like leaves, color changes in the fall
Life alters, once and for all.
Like tall trees and their branches,
Standing firmly against the wind.
No matter how misty is the sight,
No matter how hard is the rain,
Breaths of nature would still ease the pain.

Like bare trees standing there
At the foot of the riverbank,
Whistling a promise of kindness.
Images merrily mirrored in the water,
As in life, we are but
A mere reflection to one another
I smile for every tribulation that comes,
For it'll just vanish in evanescent time.

Life's a kiss of lightning!
Might as well relish each moment.
Let every heart's desire be satisfied.
Exult! Even if the clouds steal the sunlight.
For what lies ahead is never a promise.
I must appreciate all that I already hold
And celebrate the privilege that life unfolds.

21

MY PEACOCK by Robin Layne

Once
I had a piñata
loved it
almost worshiped it
hanging from the ceiling on a wire
from Mexico,
a peacock.
Then
we had a party.
We broke it.
I was afraid.
They chased me with the stumped remains,
I pressed against my bedroom door
to keep them out.

In time I ventured out,
tried to repair my peacock,
had dreams of replacing the
flowing
bright-green
tissue paper tail.

Finally I scrapped the bird
but what it stood for
I remember…
It made me smile, glowing over my bed
like an angel watching.
It was beauty.

Peacock photographed by Jean Harkin

Published in the Oregon Writer's Association Anthology 1996

HUMOR

Mufasa in the Sink photographed by Judy Beaston

ART FOR ART'S SAKE by Richard David Bach

My name is Art, and I brew sake—*Art's Sake*—I call it. My sake is the best rice wine this side of Tokyo and I predict that *Art's Sake* will be the most successful libation since Coca-Cola—provided I get the marketing right. Marketing will be crucial if *Art's Sake* is to become a best-seller in the rice wine genre.

The first thing in my marketing plan will be the bottle and the label. The label itself must be an attention-getter and I've selected the work of a noted artist for that purpose—Katsushika Hokusai's "The Great Wave off Kanagawa." That magnificent piece, perhaps the most famous of Japanese paintings, is art that will stand out, art that will remind the drinker of the origins of rice wine, and art that will attract those who buy their rice wine on the basis of how it looks on the shelf. This will be the art for *Art's Sake*.

Social media—Facebook, Twitter and Instagram—will be the marketing platform for *Art's Sake* and I will definitely employ a blog tour. I'm planning a pre-launch blitz using my extensive email and Facebook following; and ATMs (Advance Tasting Modules) of *Art's Sake* will be sent to critics—at least to those who review rice wines. (Most are in Japan.)

I've debated hiring a professional publicist to design my marketing program but I decided to do it myself at first. I've taken a number of courses on how to produce a best seller and have sat through many lectures on the subject. Most emphasize the notion that the contents of the bottle are less important than the exterior—the producer must first get members of his (or her) potential audience to take it off the shelf.

And for that, the artwork on the label should be extraordinary—just as a standout cover of a book is a must to attract readers. The "Great Wave" will do that and will be art for *Art's Sake*.

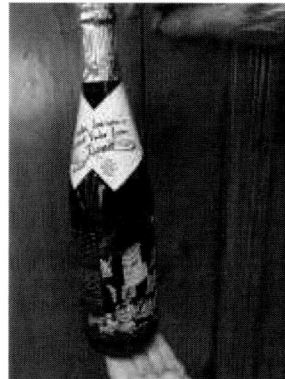

Inspired by Katsushika Hokusai's
The Great Wave off Kanagawa,

Photo by author is not Art's Sake—it's the contest award given to him for this piece of writing.

SEVENTEEN SPIDERS BEFORE I SHOWER
by Zaferia Russell

A few weeks ago I traveled to Southern California to spend some quality time with my mother for her birthday. She's a June baby—a Cancer—and in truth she is not doing very well these days. She is fragile. So I make a concerted effort to see her at least twice a year. I know I won't have many years left before she is gone.

I flew down before her birthday and was looking forward to my stay with her and the few things she can still do and loves to do—play cards and board games; go out to dinner; just sit and talk. I settled into my bedroom for the night and looked forward to my first full day with my mom.

I'm an early riser—always have been—so I crept into the bathroom to prepare for my shower. Gasp! As I organized my toiletries and other necessities I started to take note of what was on the walls and in the shower and on the ceiling above the shower—spiders. A lot of spiders. Large, long-legged really creepy spiders. They were everywhere—in the corners by the tub; behind the toilet bowl (a couple of large ones); and on the ceiling above the shower and above the sink.

Suddenly I found myself in the middle of the plot from the movie *Arachnophobia*. But which character am I? Am I the debilitated doctor whose crippling fear of spiders renders him useless until the very end of the movie or am I the John Goodman character with a large can of pesticide and a very jolly *let's kill killer spiders* persona?

Now at this point if you practice the Hindu faith or are a Buddhist, you may not want to read any further. I realize that the death of even a repulsive, eight-legged house interloper is frowned upon. But I have a different religion when it comes to insects and spiders—my religious belief says that if you are outside, you are in the right environment, belong there and I am happy to share the outdoors with you. However, if you are inside where I am living, staying or wanting to take a shower, then you are in the wrong place and thus are fair game for instant and permanent removal. I realize that this logic/religion of mine is flawed; however, it's still a free country and thus my belief system has meaning and merit for me. The process of indoor extermination for vermin will proceed.

My heart started to beat faster and maybe even skip a few beats. I have arachnophobia. It's not as bad as my daughter's fear of spiders—maybe a few notches lower—but it's definitely there. I considered my options: (1) Don't take a shower during the entire time I stay here; not a good option for me, but a possibility; (2) find another place to stay and just visit during the day; Mom would be disappointed but hopefully understanding; (3) kill all the spiders; kill them now and be quick about it.

I chose option 3, so maybe I'm part debilitated doctor and part John Goodman character from *Arachnophobia* at this point. Now the next question was how do I kill them all without any of them touching me, dropping on me, biting me or otherwise creeping the heck out of and rendering me useless, frazzled or freaked out? They say that necessity is the mother of invention; well that's true. I invented many new ways to kill spiders that morning, methodologies which were both necessary and unique.

The low easy-to-reach spiders were a no-brainer: I killed those handily with my flip-flop. Bang, bang—smashed spider guts were integrated into my flip-flop's sole. No problem. That took care of four spiders. But what about the high-looming spiders, the ones on the ceiling or located in the high corners of the room? Or the ones located behind the toilet bowl? The rounded slick surface and the awkward position in which the toilet bowl spiders were located would mean my trying to kill them while basically flying blind. Not a good idea at all, especially with my current heart rate and intensified feeling of self-preservation. Mistakes could be made.

I looked around the room for anything I could turn into a weapon of mass destruction against spiders. I spotted an orange-scented air freshener and hit on the idea if I sprayed toward the higher spiders the orange oil might make them slide down and stun them long enough for me to deploy my flip-flop. Well that worked in the short run, but then the bathroom (which had no windows) was starting to reek of orange-scented air freshener. I was feeling queasy, but had killed an additional four spiders. The death toll was now eight. But that meant nine more spiders.

I was beginning to feel a bit frenzied, like some mad spider-killing woman on a spider serial killing spree. I stopped to take a breath and wondered if this was what serial killers experienced when they went on a murderous binge. I've seen interviews of serial killers and psychologists talking about "inside the mind of a killer," and they have talked about the "killer's high," the physical relief that comes from killing; or the sense of satisfaction that some killers have talked about feeling. Others have talked about the actual physical pleasure they have experienced while killing.

It was time for me to do a self-check—was I feeling satisfied, happy or relieved from the act of eliminating eight spiders from the world? Honestly, no to all three of those questions. I felt neither relief nor pleasure nor a sense of accomplishment. I did notice that my potty-mouth had been unleashed, though. But surely that is understandable, right? I mean a half an hour later in the morning and I am not showered; I have not had my coffee yet; and I have already worked up a sweat killing these beasts. Who wouldn't utter a few curse words by this time?

Okay, since I was pretty sure I would not turn into a mass murderer after this, I needed to focus on finishing the task at hand. There were still two massive-sized spiders behind the toilet bowl and several spiders on the ceiling above the sink and the shower. A quick second survey of the room and I took notice of the coffee cup I had placed my toothbrush and toothpaste in the night I arrived from Portland. I had a new spider-killing idea!

I took the toothbrush and toothpaste out of the coffee mug and filled it with very, very hot water. I began to fling hot water at the ceiling spiders. One by one they shriveled up as they slid down the walls and into the tub or the sink. Progress. I turned on the showerhead and the now-dead spiders slid down the shower drain. Same for the sink spiders—after I was sure they were dead and not going to climb out of the sink drain and attack me in my sleep—I let them slide into sewer oblivion. Good-bye spiders.

At last I could finally take a shower. And God knows, by now I really needed one: I was dripping in sweat and still suffering from the emotional effects of killing huge spiders while keeping my fear of them in check long enough to complete the task. I think that's called post-traumatic stress syndrome, which I was hoping a spider-free shower and a good cup of coffee would cure before I could wish my still-snoring mom a good morning. She would never know—because she doesn't need to know—that her daughter had to battle seventeen spiders that morning before she could be clean and fresh.

I heard rustling from my mom's bedroom. She was getting up. I dressed and went into the kitchen to make us some coffee. "Good morning," my mom said, as she very slowly small-stepped her way to the breakfast table.

"Good morning, Mom. Would you like a cup of coffee?"

"I would love one," she replied. "Did you sleep well?"

"Yup, perfectly," I replied.

"I see you have showered—did you have plenty of hot water?"

"Yes, Mom, plenty of hot water. The shower was blissful. Thank you."

UNMENTIONABLE TERM by Lauri Leonetti

You are conceivably a remarkable word: suggesting sounds and sights, one in particular, awakening new thoughts and memories, evoking fresh ideas and archaic idioms, but creating angst in me. I used to hope and wait and wonder. Perhaps my chance has passed, so now I choose to ignore you—oh, you ambivalent term!

Of course, once I try to block the reminders, you're everywhere.

The neighbor drives by, windows open on a summer afternoon, her child singing along with a nursery rhyme tune. Now I hate rosies and pockets full of posies.

I turn on the television to an educational show. You're the star when the logger fells a tree to read the tally of time, and when the astronomer gazes as you festoon Saturn.

A quick remote command, and I'm viewing an ad. On behalf of the acrobats, clowns and lions, Barnum and Bailey will bring three of you for spectators to view.

I switch the channel again, where a gymnast hangs from you to swing and twirl and spin.

One more try with another station, when I watch you support a boxer as he rebounds to knock out his rival. When the announcer previews a wrestling match to follow, I surrender.

Turning to chores for distraction, I find you on the coffee table, discarded by a coaster-less cup, then circling a shirt collar in my laundry, and sneaking around my bathtub dressed as soap scum, below my towel, draped in your clutch.

With food, I'm not safe either. You hug my napkin, I see you in my doughnut, and as I rummage in my cupboard, you beckon from the mold hoping to transform jello or cake batter into your form.

Before leaving the house, I look at myself in the mirror, but can't escape you there. You're the dark surrounding my eyes, like a racoon, and the decoration in my ear lobes. My sister walks up behind me, and the reflection shows you embellishing her eyebrow as well.

I plan a reprieve with a trip to the fair. What was I thinking? You're holding my keys. I go anyway, but then I meet you in the snouts of parading pigs, and leading the bulls. I cannot avoid the shape of their arena, nor the dogs running in you to corral the sheep.

As I try to escape, I pass booths which create your outline again, the animal barns clustered in your center. A Native American, following the archetype of her ancestors, forms a smoky demonstration of communicating with you in the sky, and kids win stuffed animals by tossing you onto milk bottles.

Heading back home, I pass a church, when a bell bids your call of the six o'clock hour, and just when I think you can plague me no more, you use my phone to taunt me further. The shrill tones cease, yet you continue to resound in my ears.

I don't care if you're familiar or true, gold or silver or brass. You may bring curtains up or down, start a new year, or end the day. Someone else may toss their hat in, but I will keep you at bay. To my deserted heart, you deserve your vile association with drugs and crime.

Wait a minute. I may reconsider. Is that you alerting me to my lost love at the door? You gain a bit more favor as you encircle our mound of mud-pie ice cream with chocolate sauce, and you're back in my good graces—my chance has come at last—when you adorn my finger with diamonds at my beloved's request.

Sorry, dear ring. You're more than remarkable, you're brilliant.

Ring photographed by Carolyn Adams

WHAT GOOGLE DIDN'T KNOW by Sheila Deeth

It was a dark and stormy night... but that was a good two days ago. The storm had passed. This bright and peaceful afternoon was clear, the traffic light, and the predicted travel time for our journey a mere, slight fifteen minutes. Alas, Google's "green road" prediction with zero delays proved sadly unfounded. Slow and languid ground to stormily stationary, and our driver, fingering a motionless steering wheel, demanded his passenger finger her phone where, on Google, she learned the road had turned to red, well-adorned with warning triangles for "incidents" ahead.

"No problem," said the driver, checking his watch as if the disaster were truly, terribly severe. "Google's bound to give an alternative route." Which, aided by the passenger's fingers on the phone, Google did. Google spoke, so we turned at the next exit, proceeding cross-country toward that other green route we would have taken if the freeway weren't faster. This proved to be a very green route. A very, very green route, winding through very green trees. Since half the freeway traffic appeared to be guided by Google, this also soon became a rather slow route. Meanwhile our light, bright afternoon deepened to dark and stormy, and probably night. We wondered, where did that weather come from? Then... wait a minute... where did that "Road closed" sign come from as well.

Google still insisted on coloring the road ahead green, with light to average traffic. Perhaps it was right—that non-existent traffic was surely light. But from where we sat, the road was blocked and black.

We followed a scarily narrow diversion, directed by half-obscured signs until Google, with computerized confidence, told us to turn, slipping and sliding down a slalom of ice slopes through suburbs of gorgeously decorated mansions, each with its own four-wheel-drive suburban guarding the space by its gate.

Google knew best, of course—of course! Google directed us back to the green and traffic-free, blocked and black road which, we learned (from Google, but not from Google maps), had been closed for two days already due to trees which fell during that long-gone dark and stormy night. So of course there was no traffic! Meanwhile our own night grew darker and stormier, inside and outside the car. Our driver clutched his steering wheel with ever-whitening fingers. His passenger clutched her seat-belt. And the road was green and brown with trunks blown down and branches blown all around. "Watch out!"

We made it through, swore at Google a lot, and learned that, after all, our internet friend really doesn't know everything. Never trust a computer, or a phone, or a passenger I suppose. The driver, supremely confident again and not white-knuckled at all, insisted he would never have made that mistake if "someone" hadn't told him to.

Signs photographed by Jean Harkin

THE GRUDGE STORE by Richard David Bach

ARE YOU HOLDING A GRUDGE,
BUT DON'T KNOW WHAT TO DO WITH IT?
WE CAN HELP.

Grudgestore.con is the online repository for those who are carrying Grudges but don't have the time or space to hold their Grudges themselves. Our satisfied customers select the level at which each Grudge is to be maintained, from an intense boil to a low simmer, with an option to slowly cool to room temperature. We have a cryogenic unit for those who wish long-term cold storage, and microwave reheat capability in the event a dormant Grudge requires rekindling.

Our flat-rate annual membership comes with the privilege of reviewing each Grudge once every 90 days to ensure that the Grudge is intact, valid and worthwhile retaining. Additional visits and revisions are available at small additional fees, and we have quantity discounts for those with multiple Grudges.

Grudgestore.con maintains the highest level of security to ensure that your Grudge is protected against unauthorized access, and in order to avoid conflicts of interest we will not allow one Grudge Store client to hold a Grudge against another client in our safe facility. Customers are required to select a complex alpha/numeric/symbol password available only to the customer but—mindful that many Grudges can survive over generations—we will work with approved family members who might inherit the Grudge upon the demise of the original Grudge Holder. And, of course, a Grudge may be returned to its owner at any time or we will, at an owner's written request, expose the Grudge to light and air in which event it will simply evaporate.

Our team of social scientists has recently published a paper in the *Journal of Idiopathic Syndromes* on the subject of "Grudge Holding and Its Impact on Health," and our CEO has published a book entitled *The Grudge: Your Place or Mine?* Chapters include "How To Identify a Grudge Worth Holding," "Is It Best To Hold One's Own Grudge," "What To Do When The Grudge Cools" and "Sex and the Single Grudge."

For more information and an application form visit our website at www.grudgestore.con or contact us at info@grudgestore.con.

TWO CHAIRS ON A BEACH

Chairs at Cannon Beach photographed by Jean Harkin

TWO CHAIRS AT SEASIDE by Jean Harkin

Two chairs looking out to sea
What are they thinking?
What can two chairs really see?
Is the sky sinking?

Two chairs perch by the seaside
Gazing toward sunset.
The ocean spans so blue and wide
The danger they forget.

Two chairs hold, the sand shifting
The pair wish to stay;
They feel the tide lifting
And soon float away.

Oregon Coast photographed by Steven Deeth

THE DUPRASS by Robin Layne

"I've found a description for *us*," Herb whispered to Marsha one morning as they sat together over oatmeal and eggs.

Marsha peeked over her newspaper onto Herb's open paperback.

Herb pointed to one word on the page and read aloud, "*Duprass*." He added the definition the novelist, Kurt Vonnegut, had coined: "A *karass* composed of only two persons."

Marsha laughed. Herb had already read to her from *Cat's Cradle* that *karasses* were groups of people that unknowingly do God's will. She leaned in for a kiss. "I know what I'm doing," she said. "Loving you—forever."

"The concept fits us so well," her husband said. "Who else do we have? No children, no pets. No close friends."

Marsha chimed in, "You're enough for me."

"And you for me," Herb pronounced, feeling like they were renewing their vows for the hundredth time.

They made sandwiches and packed them into a basket with cheese, rye crackers, fruit, and a bottle of wine. Herb hung the basket over his left arm and then grasped his wife's shoulder. The two helped each other up the path to the beach. When they passed the old white sign whose headline read, "Beware of sneaker waves," Marsha snuck her free hand up and tickled Herb's armpit. Herb felt as if they were miles away from the danger of undertows or anything else.

Every morning, Herb and Marsha walked down the path to the beach, where they sat together on two padded dining room chairs and spent the day holding hands and looking out at the sea. Sometimes the waves flowed dreamlike in and out and gulls mewed overhead. Other times, breakers thundered and beachcombers fled the threatening rain. As long as weather allowed, the *duprass* stayed put through the subtle or brilliant colors of sunset. They took turns leading in a prayer: "Dear Lord, thank You for Your beautiful world. Thank You for saving our souls. Thank You that we have each other. When we go, please let us go together. Neither of us can imagine living without the other."

Their days at the beach in their fading chairs ebbed as they struggled with increasing health problems. Herb had a double bypass but insisted on taking what walks he could to watch the waves and sky with his beloved. Marsha's knee cartilages wore down; her doctor said she would have to lose forty pounds before a surgeon could replace them. But the couple loved sitting together, having their daily picnic.

On a sunny fall day, they picked their way through crackling fallen leaves past the sneaker wave sign. Both used canes with their free hands. This time, their food was meager because their appetites had worn thin.

When they looked at each other, their long-held affection stirred. They kissed as if they had never kissed before. A rare high tide crept in, lapping at the front legs of the two chairs. Then a breaker beneath the water slipped up and took the couple under.

It was all so fast, so unexpected. One moment they were in the shallows, Herb reaching for Marsha's hand, foot, anything, slipping, and then driftwood knocked him deeper, oh, and lungs so aching, filling with water—something struck his head so brutally it knocked him out.

***

The pain was also over fast. Herb was now in a shining new place. A glorious Presence permeated the air. He could move freely, without his body resisting or hurting. Without glasses, he could see for miles: People with auras of varying brightness walked on shimmering gold roads, smelling flowers more brilliant than any on earth; angels walked with them... but where was Marsha?

He felt a presence beside him, and turned to see an angel—breathtakingly tall and strong, with wings sweeping out behind his back. "Please, sir," Herb said. "Where is she? I was sure Heaven couldn't be Heaven without her. I can't imagine the gates being closed to her. But—if for any reason she's not here, I'll go find her. I'd scour Hell to get my wife!"

The angel looked at Herb as if anticipating more.

"Do I—need to go higher up for an explanation? Or—permission to..." The beauty of Heaven was getting to him, but something was all wrong. He searched his own heart. "I don't deserve to be here. Perhaps you can—put in a word for her? Tell them I'll go down if she can come up here? She deserves a reward more than I do!"

A flicker of a smile from the angel encouraged him.

With deeper soul searching, he realized that neither he nor Marsha deserved Heaven. They had loved one another well, but they had shut everyone else out of their *duprass*.

Herb fell to his knees. "Lord, have mercy on a sinner!" he cried. "I thought we were good people. We didn't cheat, lie, steal, or kill. But neither did we take care of the poor, the homeless, or the lonely. Why am I even here?"

At last the angel spoke: "By the mercy of God. He gave you the faith to trust His Son's dear sacrifice for you. There was so much more He wanted to do *with* you and *through* you. God wants you to know He is a *karass* of three— less limited than a *duprass*."

Herb was surprised that Heaven would use terms invented in Vonnegut's novel.

"It was easy for you to love Marsha," the angel continued. "Others who loved when it was hard to love now shine here like stars. Rise. Your Lord is coming to wipe every tear from your eyes." He pulled Herb back to his feet.

Herb realized he had been weeping. He thought about the times Marsha had wiped his tears. Was it improper for him to inquire about his own wife? Even if it was, he had to know… "What about Marsha?" he asked.

"I'm here," came a voice behind him.

He turned to see Marsha. She was sobbing. He took her hand.

Flanked by two angels, they made their way toward the brightest glow in the distance.

Herb and Marsha Robin Layne

EMPTY HEART by Judy Beaston

What if I never met Jason on a quiet January night
What if he walked away that night, never called again
What if I accepted the teaching post in Michigan
What If I didn't follow him to San Diego
What if we chose a childless union
What if our son loved music and not the surf
What if the ocean wasn't in need of another body
What if I only ever had one beach chair
What if I turned away when Jason had an affair
What if I flew away from San Diego
What if I moved back to Michigan
What if I never met Jason
Would I be happy then?
Would my heart be full?
Would I know peace?
What if…

Depoe Bay photographed by Sheila Deeth

THE PACT by Karen Alexander-Brown

Pat stares out from the squad car's windows at the two semi-silhouetted high-backed wooden beach chairs in the middle of the sand facing the beginnings of a cloudy sunset. The gulls are resting at the water's edge, wings all tucked and still after the day's scavenging for food. Pat rests her left wrist on the steering wheel and removes her cap to scratch her short thatch of mouse-colored hair with her right hand. This is her favorite time of the day, but her mood is disturbed tonight.

Florence Beach photographed by Carolyn Adams

The scene on the beach is peaceful now, but just last evening the area had been a swirl of activity around those two chairs. The sand leading up to and around them is all churned and broken by a crowd of footprints. It had been Marge and Merv's 50th wedding anniversary and the tiny coastal town had turned out to celebrate its much-loved elders.

39

The wary attention of the resting birds shifts suddenly. Movement on the beach catches Pat's eye. She recognizes Eric, the teen who had made the 911 call last night. His shoulders scrunched inside his jacket against the cool air, he advances with a furtive determination toward the two chairs planted in the sand. Once there he kneels and pulls some red, white and blue carnations from inside his jacket. Placing them on the sand, he digs a small hole in front of the chairs and places the carnations in it, carefully scooping sand into the hole around the stems to hold the flowers in place. Then he rises, brushes off his hands, looks around at the empty beach and skulks away. A moment later the silhouetted figures of a mother and young daughter walk down to the chairs to leave a teddy bear and some ribbon-tied daisies on the seats. They stand a few moments after depositing their offerings on the empty chairs and the mother says something to her daughter. At this distance, what is said is inaudible to Pat. As they leave hand in hand, the girl starts skipping playfully at her mother's side, evidently satisfied at having fulfilled the task.

Pat smiles and shakes her head at the oblivious optimism of youth. Suddenly snippets of her post-mortem interrogations return and play again in her head.

"No, they were always loving with each other," said the couple's neighbor this morning, setting down a hot cup of coffee on the kitchen table for Pat. "They joked about their infirmities with a sense of humor. He had trouble walking, all bent over and depending upon a walker for balance. She was in better shape, but her arthritis got in the way so I helped out sometimes. They had no children or relatives that I know of. Still, I envied them for their loving relationship. All those years together!"

"They always seemed happy," observed the local market cashier. "We used to see them in town shopping or out on their walks. That is, until he became less mobile. Someone said he was diagnosed with terminal cancer or something."

Eric had been the last to see them. He had volunteered to help bag up and remove the trash after the celebration. It was at about this time of the evening and the last of the revelers had headed home. Marge and Merv had asked to remain on the beach and Eric had promised everyone that he would keep an eye out for them in case they needed him.

"They were just sitting there, holding hands and talking quietly. I was lugging the bags over to the jeep. After a couple of trips to the car I saw her stand and help him up. They hugged. I asked if they wanted a ride back home, but they just smiled, waved and said, 'No thanks.' Then they started walking toward the overlook. I thought they were going to watch the waves, but when I returned from the jeep the last time they were gone. Just disappeared!"

The rescue teams had found their battered and soggy bodies at the base of the rocks that lead down to the mouth of the river as it empties into the ocean. It took a couple of hours to get them up the rocks and into the ambulance. By then the fishing boats were finishing up their catch and heading back to the wharfs.

Pat opens up her thermos and takes another swig of coffee laced with creamer. She replaces the thermos cap and tucks it into the car door holder. Starting up the engine she sighs and thinks to herself, "Will I be alone when I die? Who will hold my hand as I go?"

She shifts into gear and the crunch of the wheels reminds her however that she still has time before that day arrives. The chairs are barely visible as darkness makes its final descent and Pat drives away, headlights slicing through the inky blue toward home.

CHAPTER 1 - *A Day In The Life Of Two Chairs Or How To Go Rogue And Live On The Beach* by Zaferia Russell

I smiled when I came upon the two formal dining chairs sitting side by side at the beach, as though they were holding hands, gazing out to sea. Of course I knew these two chairs. Intimately. The last time I saw them was at my best friend's house. We were just sitting down to a very formal dinner party—ladies in evening gowns, men in suits and ties. But that was twenty years ago. The chairs had weathered the test of time rather well: fabric still beautifully intact, no scratches on the lovely cherry wooden frames.

I had been with Louise when she picked them out. Picking out furniture was a real thing for Weezy (my affectionate nickname for her). In fact, just window-shopping on Montana Avenue in Santa Monica was a big deal. Oh my, how she did love to window-shop in all those high-end stores. She would whisper to me, as we walked along Montana Avenue on any given Saturday, "Do you know who I saw shopping on Montana the other day?" "Who?" I replied, though I knew it was going to be some well-known actress or actor. Santa Monica was piled high to the sky with the well-known of Hollywood. Pacific Palisades, too. And right down the street from Santa Monica and Pacific Palisades was Malibu, the crown jewel of beach communities to the rich and famous. For there lived Barbra Streisand, Johnny Carson and dozens of others, both A-and-B-listers. I wondered who she had seen that caused her to speak in such reverent hushed tones. Must be somebody good.

"Sally Fields," she replied. "She was in the lingerie store—picking out camisoles." "Wow," I said, "that's amazing." (I tried to express the *Wow* in an equally-reverent hushed tone, but I knew I didn't even come close.) For me, seeing a *movie star* is no big deal. When I was little, I saw movie stars all the time: Bob Hope, Jimmy Durante, Danny Kaye—and a bunch of other *funny men*. You might ask why that would be the case. The truth is my mom was a comedy writer for quite a few *funny men* in Hollywood. Mostly, she had worked for Bob Hope, writing material for him for his USO Shows, some radio bits that he did and various and sundry other TV appearances.

She wrote for him from about the early 1950s through the very early 1960s. Since my mom was a single parent and a working mom, she often dragged me and my brother along to her work meetings. Of course, it didn't help that her work was unconventional, with all that that implies— unconventional hours, working on the weekends, attending evening or late afternoon awards shows or programs. Being dragged to Bob Hope's home in

Silver Lake when I was a kid, just so he could practice punch lines that my mom had written for him, was not a picnic for me or my brother. Needless to say, I was neither interested in my mom's work, nor was Bob Hope particularly fond of other people's children. Mostly, we just tried to stay off his radar; in other words, be as invisible as possible, so that my mom could get done with work and spend time with us.

But back to Louise and those exquisite chairs, longingly gazing out to sea. I know Louise put them there; it was her way of making a dramatic statement. She always was very dramatic. Perhaps she should have gone into acting, rather than looking for movie stars who might be walking around the Santa Monica Promenade or shopping the high-end stores of Montana Avenue. When I met Louise for the first time, she was dating my brother. It was 1985. Dating my brother was her first mistake. Falling for him was her second mistake. Moving in with him was her third mistake.

As ever, I bit my tongue and mentally wished her the best in her pursuit of a romantic relationship with Basil. But nobody knows your family like you know your family, and what I know about my brother would fill volumes. More to the point, he is what young folks these days call *a player*. Never have I ever known my brother to be faithful to any one woman. Ever. So you can imagine my trepidation when he introduced Louise to me as his girlfriend. I liked her from the get-go; yet I was already mentally preparing myself for the day when she would come crying on my shoulder to tell me that she found out Basil was cheating on her.

Surprisingly that day came nearly nine years later. The surprise was not that he had cheated on her; no, of course not. The surprise was that it took him so long to do so. Or to be caught doing so. They had been dating for about a year or so when Louise gave up her apartment and moved in with my brother. Things between them were good for a very long time. I mean, really, really good. The love and affection were there; Louise was getting the kind of attention from Basil that led me to believe, gee, maybe Louise is *the one* for him. They might get married. I could have Louise for my sister-in-law! I thought the world of her: She is kind, funny and generous, and a lady in every sense of the word. As the years went by and they were still together, I was so happy for the two of them. We socialized together constantly—my husband and I with Louise and Basil. We got very close. Somewhere along the line she became more than my friend, she was family to me. Louise became the sister I had longed for as a child.

There was no going back; no matter what happened between Louise and Basil, she would always be my *adopted* sister and my best friend. And just about the time I had let my guard down and started to believe they would be together forever, the betrayal hit the fan. Royally. It started with an errant VISA receipt she found in his pocket; but it was a receipt that raised a red flag. She hadn't been looking for it, of course. She found it in the everyday routine of living; she found it when she was doing the laundry.

Why is it always a VISA receipt that gives you guys away? Hadn't Basil watched any Lifetime Movie Network movies? You know the ones, the weepy kind with scorned women or betrayed women running around with knives or guns in their purses, wanting revenge. Geez. This was going to be a hard breakup and I knew no matter what I did—whether it was to comfort Louise or scold Basil for his callous behavior—there would be no going back. Their relationship, if it was to be salvaged on any level, would never be the same. And I wondered, would Louise still want to be my friend or would I just be another painful reminder of an ugly and hard breakup?

Chair photographed by Carolyn Adams

DARK AND STORMY

Photograph by Judy Beaston

REFUGE by Karen Alexander-Brown

In the flash of white light that fluttered for an instant through the rain-spattered window she saw the silhouette of the woman in a long robe-like dress cut into graph-like squares by the window's white wood slats. The dark shape was momentarily backlit by dense gray fog. The figure seemed to be crushing a smaller bundle to its chest—perhaps a child? A tremendous roll of thunder followed shortly thereafter. She shuddered, unsure of whether to close the curtains or to open the door and invite the woman inside.

Another flash revealed silhouettes of other figures joining the woman and bundle, that of a man with a young child clinging to his leg. Again the foggy backlighting erased their features and made them into dark statuesque shapes outlined in the momentary light. Then everything disappeared in the darkness of the night.

She felt vulnerable, alone in her home with her husband away on a business trip. Looking around the dimly lit living room she perceived the comforting shapes of the cushy brown leather sofas arranged in an L-shape that framed the edges of a Native American patterned wool rug, rough-hewn log furniture completing the rustic southwestern feel of the room. A fire danced in the gas-lit fireplace, warming the space. She waited for a knock on the door or another flash of lightning, but only the pounding of the rain on the roof cut through the dense silence. Would they go away on their own?

She reached for her cell phone, but service was spotty and she couldn't call anyone. The landline and the internet had been down for days. At times like these, she questioned the self-sufficiency of their rural location. However her husband had dreamed of owning his own vineyard so they had moved to the outskirts of Dundee, Oregon, upon retirement. He still maintained contact with his associates and sometimes did occasional consulting work.

Another flash and almost simultaneously the thunder rolled. The silhouettes had increased in numbers, almost filling the sloping front yard it seemed, although she could only guess at their number from her vantage point a small distance from the front window. Suddenly she felt a panicked burst of anger inside, a sense of being trapped in her own home. Cozy comfort became cloying claustrophobia.

"Go away!" she shouted, at first haltingly, then with more force and volume. "GO AWAY!"

Immediately the thunder clapped a loud roar and she was overcome with guilt. How un-Christian was her behavior? These people were in the cold wet rain. Perhaps they needed help. Where did they come from? Why were they gathered in front of her house? How many did the neighbors (who were few and far between) receive, and did they receive them?

She placed her left hand upon the door handle, a fluted French wing somewhat out-of-place with the rest of the décor. The fingers of her right hand grasped the smaller wing to open the bolt when another flash of lightning caused her to press her body against the heavy wood paneled door. In that instant she perceived a crush of silhouettes outside and hands pressed against the wet surface of the window.

"What am I doing? What do I do?" she asked herself under her rapid breath. She waited for the thunderclap, but it did not come for several tense seconds, and when it did it sounded far away.

Peeling herself from the surface of the door, she slid herself along the periphery of the room and dashed across the kitchen while glancing at the darkened windows there. She moved down the stairs to the unfinished basement area in which they stored their supplies and mementos, clicking on the single light bulb before she descended. On a high shelf she found the long case covered in dust and the smaller case heavy with ammunition.

She loaded the hunting rifle with fumbling fingers. She did not feel comfortable with arms, but her husband had felt it necessary to teach her how to load and fire the rifle. She struggled with the mechanisms, wondering whether she was over-reacting to the situation or not.

Once up the stairs, she cautiously approached the dark window and waited. The rain pounded with less intensity, but the storm continued. Where to put the rifle, she wondered. She couldn't just aim it at them in hostility as she assessed their intentions, but she wanted it nearby and accessible. Finally she decided to balance it against the wall, out of view alongside the doorframe, but within reach of her right hand.

She placed her hands on the doorknob and wing for the bolt and turned the wing slowly. She pulled open the door just a tad to peer out with one eye.

The yard was empty. She pulled the door wide open and switched on the porch light. Nothing. No one. Pulling up the throw she had over her shoulders in order to cover her head against the rain, she walked a few steps into the darkness. She glanced at the window to her left for clues. Nothing.

Once more facing the darkness, she noticed a crumpled shape out on the gravel pathway that led to the door. She winced against the raindrops pelting her face and eyes and walked toward the shape. Leaning down, she gingerly lifted a sopping baby blanket off the gravel, all filthy with mud and wear, the animal shapes in blues and pinks and yellows indecipherable in its condition. Its edges were ripped and hanging.

She stood and turned this way and that, but in the darkness she could only just make out the outlines of the surrounding hillsides. She walked back toward the front door listening to the crunch of wet gravel beneath her boots as her back hunched against the rain. That is when she saw the note stuck flat and wet against the lower left window panel. With trepidation she approached it and leaned in. Something was written in coarse block letters that were bleeding toward illegibility. She took off and wiped her glasses with an inside edge of the throw.

"WHY DO YOU FEAR US? WE ARE JUST LIKE YOU" was written on it.

The salt of her tears mixed with the rain on her cheeks. She dropped the filthy rain-soaked blanket under the window and crumpled up the soggy note in her fist. Then she went inside to sit by the fire and dry off in silence, enclosed in her thoughts.

Dark Clouds photographed by Karen Alexander-Brown

AN EXTRAORDINARY DAY by Jessie Collins

Sometimes, what begins as a perfectly ordinary day can turn into something quite extraordinary. I was visiting my daughter, and we had planned to spend the morning shopping—the sort of *mother and daughter* activity that is particularly pleasant when the two people concerned live far apart and don't get to do it very often. Off we went, on a cold but dry and sunny morning, and enjoyed ourselves until it was time to return home for lunch. As we ate our meal, we noticed a change in the weather. The sun had disappeared behind a bank of clouds, and little snowflakes were idly drifting down.

My daughter had arranged to pick up one of her sons at the train station and take him to see the doctor, with whom he had an early afternoon appointment. I was going to go with them, as I hadn't seen my grandson for some time. However, the snow began to come down in earnest and the clouds looked distinctly stormy. We decided it would be more sensible for me to stay indoors, and it wouldn't be for long, as the whole trip should last for no more than a couple of hours.

Off she went, and I settled down with a book. I am noted for switching off the outside world completely when I get absorbed in reading a good story, and I was quite startled when the phone rang. It was my grandson, telling me not to worry that his mother would be back later than planned. The heavy snowfall was causing problems on the roads and they were making slow progress, but she should be home by about 4:30 pm.

I realized as I looked out of the window that the afternoon was progressing toward what would evidently be a dark and stormy night, but I wasn't too concerned just then, because my daughter was going to be home before it went properly dark. However, much worse was to follow.

At about 5:00 pm my grandson phoned again, to say that they were still hopelessly stuck in traffic and it might be about 6:30 pm before his mother got home. Soon afterward my son-in-law arrived home early from work and immediately set about clearing a quantity of snow from the drive. By this time, I was getting worried, but he said he was sure she would be fine, although we wouldn't hear from her because she would be alone in the car after dropping the boy at the station. It really was a dark and stormy night by now, and as time went on I was panicking.

There was another phone call at about 7:30 pm. The poor girl was in a long, stationary queue at traffic lights quite close to home, but both she and the car were perfectly okay. Then at long last, about 8:15 pm, she rushed into the house, aiming for the bathroom, having sat for six hours in the car.

I wouldn't like another day like that in a hurry.

IN WINTER'S HUSH by Carolyn Adams

I walk a quiet avenue,
the night woven with
deep-throated bells:
a call to worship
or to mourning.
The last of a storm,
its push of fallen leaves
to season's end,
calls me to pursue the hour.
I pass curtained windows,
the laughter of children
and their prayers
against the odd, hulking stranger.
Trees, soon to bud and bloom,
whisper in winter's hush
of another riotous spring.
On broken sidewalks,
I leave the lit path
for outbound streets.

The wind foretells my leaving;
the silence ponders my return.

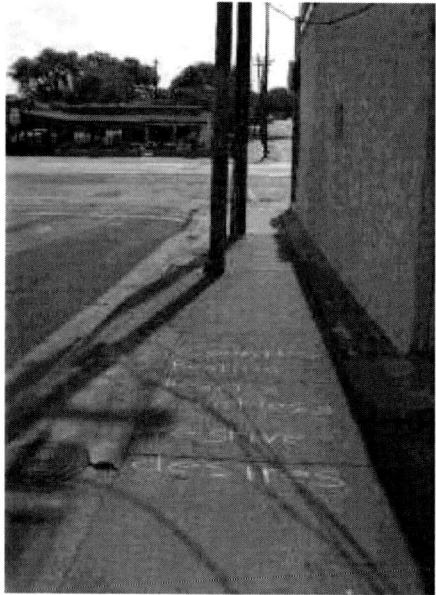

Countless Beating Hearts photographed by Carolyn Adams

A DARK AND STORMY KNIGHT by Robin Layne

Once as I sat at my studies, I felt a dark and stormy knight pounding on the castle door. His raucous mind so clouded mine, I dropped my lesson slate and forgot what I had been doing. I shook my head hard, trying to clear it—but confusion and dread poured over me. I saw his hand as clearly as if it were my own—a huge hand in a black gauntlet. *I'm coming to destroy you, you horrible, unnatural girl!* he screamed. *You have no power against me! After you're tortured, I'll tear you limb from limb!*

Pound! Pound! Pound!

Let me in, or we'll torture all your household, then find your parents and put such an end to them, the tale will terrorize children for ages!

My foster mother ran to me. I gazed at her but couldn't hear her thoughts—in fact, I couldn't even think of her name. She stared at me, saying something, but for once I was grateful I'm deaf. The noise in my head would have been even louder if her voice had joined it through ears that worked.

The knight's dark mind pulled at mine, wrenching secrets that I somehow had no ability to hold in: the faces and names of my real father and mother; the house where I had lived with them, before I was taken to this castle because... *Aha!* he blustered. *Now I know for certain you're the one who paths more strongly than any other! But I'm strong in many ways, and I will stop you.*

From what? I telepathed to him.

The lady was looking at me with deep concern. Couldn't she hear the man pounding at the door? Where were the guards? Didn't they know this knight had come with evil intent? Why had the lady run to *me*?

She grasped my hand and looked into my eyes. Her thoughts broke through the painful cacophony: *Beryl! Why are you screaming?*

I'm screaming? I pathed.

I've never heard such sounds from you. To my surprise, she held me close. *What ails you?*

The man at the castle gate's flooding my mind with so many thoughts I can't do a thing!

We haven't heard anyone out there.

The inner storm made me panic. I shook my head again, tempted to bang it against the wall in hope of stilling the invasion. *It's stormy, milady! Sounds like a hurricane—feels like a siege!*

Child, the weather is fair today! Look out the window. She led me to one. I saw a blue sky with two birds flapping by.

51

There's a big knight in black armor—a powerful man threatening to destroy us. He fills my mind with his being. It's—ugly. So wrathful! What will he do to us?

You think he's coming here?

I thought he was already *here.*

Beryl, the only person we're expecting today is Dodd, a lad about your age.

The lad will be in danger if the knight finds him.

I'll send soldiers to look for this dangerous dark knight, and to escort the lad. Is the knight by himself?

She trembled, still holding me, not getting help. I felt tears on her cheeks. Her thoughts were speeding up; she was picking up my panic. I struggled to bury the emotions that made it hard for her to act. She needed to provide a haven for me and for Dodd… Haven. Yes. That was her name. I pathed her name, but still she clung to me. So I pulled away from her, saying with my expression that it was necessary. At last, she nodded and ran off calling for help.

I was buried in the hour's torment. The threats became images: Mother would be dragged behind the knight's huge horse, hitting stones and tree roots along the road, and screaming, *What have we done? Who let this man know where we live?* I winced. He knew it because I had just revealed it to him. I lowered my head. Would she be injured beyond recovery? Would I ever see Mother again?

I saw soldiers marching through the woods with the knight. If we didn't open the drawbridge, they would surely besiege us. I felt our best defense was to keep them from reaching the castle.

He sent me an image of a youth with long black hair grabbing me and hauling me into a dungeon. The youth glared at me, sending such degrading feelings I knew he had worse plans for me than the knight had for my mother… I fought the images, sending the knight random thoughts to keep him from overwhelming me or realizing Lady Haven was ordering an ambush. I barely thought about what I was doing as I rushed to my room, wrapped a cloak over my gown, then crept through a secret passage that went under the moat and took me outside. I didn't want my foster parents to worry about me, but I was determined to face the black knight alone. It took all my concentration to block all images of the secret exit so he couldn't use it to get in. This knight would surely regret threatening me ahead of time!

I took my favorite dirt path through the woods, wondering how to reach Dodd privately. I prayed to the Child of the Star that I would find the boy and protect him. I wondered why the knight wanted to attack us all. *What have I ever done against you?*

It's what you would *do,* he broke into my thoughts, *against my young Lord Randamir.* I had never heard of Randamir, but instantly the image of the youth who would haul me into the dungeon returned. My stomach wrenched as I realized that youth was the authority behind this black-armored knight. If the knight were not stopped, I would be forced to meet the more hazardous Randamir. *What you would do,* the knight went on, *if we did not break you first.*

Then, in front of me, at a fork in the dirt path, I saw a boy shorter than me, his head covered by a hood. I could tell by his open, moving mouth that he was talking loudly. But I could hear no thoughts from him. He looked around, and then he walked toward me. I made out the name "Dodd" on his lips as he gestured toward his chest.

You're in terrible danger! I pathed. *And... I am, too.* It had been foolish to leave the castle alone. My courage withered. Dodd looked so small and weak, I worried for both of us. And why wasn't he responding to my thoughts?

You—we're both in danger, I repeated.

He looked at my wide eyes, and spoke again. But I heard no thoughts. This time I knew it wasn't because the knight was overwhelming my mind. I was getting better at blocking that man somehow. I sensed the evil knight was drawing close, however. What was wrong with Dodd? The idea that he was incapable of thinking sprang to mind. Such an idea must surely insult him! But he didn't look put off by it. There was no time to ask why Lady Haven was taking him in, whether he had some special talent to hone, like my telepathic strength. I focused on his face, trying to make out his words by sight.

His hood slipped off, revealing short clumps of light-brown hair with bald spots. He blushed and replaced the hood.

I pointed to my ears and shook my head. "I—can't—hear," I said; I wasn't sure I succeeded in speaking aloud, because I couldn't hear the echo in his mind.

Through the knight's mind, I heard the loud crunch of boots. The lad jumped, looking alarmed. He glanced behind him. Then he faced me, blushing even deeper. He mouthed, *I—can't—path.*

He couldn't telepath? How strange! Everyone in Hoteree, and in all the known world, was a telepath.

I grabbed Dodd's hand, to lead him someplace where we could hide.

Suddenly, I experienced something so odd it frightened me at first. Then... perfect peace. It was something other people described feeling late at night when everyone nearby was asleep. I had never had this profound experience; my mind had always picked up someone's thoughts somewhere. This something was divine. It was... silence.

It was so profound I could have enjoyed it for hours—but that would have cost both our lives.

"Dodd? Come." I hated speaking aloud, interrupting this moment of paradise. But it was the only way his silent mind could hear me. "Let's hide. Between your silence and my extreme pathing, we'll find a way to defeat this dark knight."

Four of Robin's Hoteree stories were dramatized on stage by Well Arts, Portland, Oregon, in What's Important Is the Story *in 2012.*

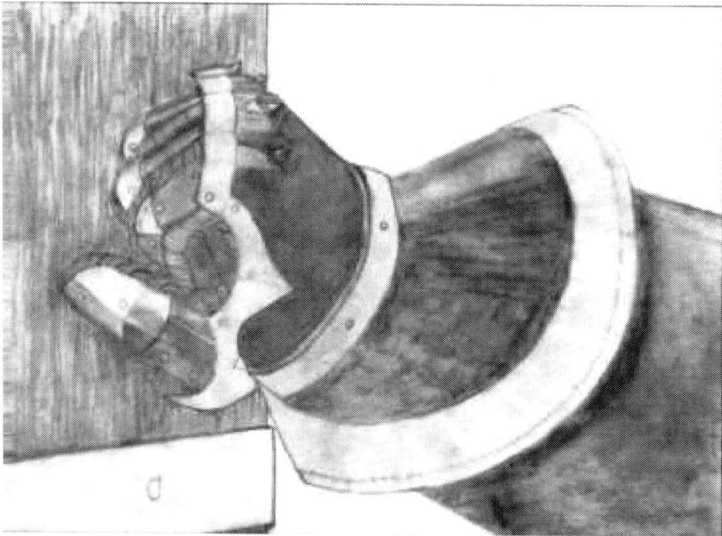

The Black Gauntlet by Robin Layne

UMBRELLA GO ROUND by Lauri Leonetti

I slipped my feet into new high heels, which my sister had insisted I buy, gazed into the mirror to check the uncomfortably-heavy layers of eyeshadow and mascara, and reached for one of my dangling earrings. As I inserted the post into my pierced ear, I heard the muffled slam of a car door. It sounded close, so I went to the window to check the driveway—empty, except for some leaves skittering across it in the wind.

I surveyed the darkening street. My husband, Karl, walked into our bedroom, interrupting me. Seeing him in jeans and a sweatshirt, I envied his comfy attire for the evening, since I'd confined my midsection in Spanx, and condemned my feet to torture. I immediately stopped that victim thinking. Because I rarely dress up, I also sensed a fluttering under that Spanx. When Karl said, "Wow, Lizzie! Don't you look awesome," I dropped my angst, and focused on having a special time with my sister, Jackie, at the symphony.

"Are you gonna wear your raincoat?" Karl asked. "When I took the dog out, I could feel the storm coming."

Twirling in front of the mirror, watching the sparkly deep-blue and gold skirt glint, I frowned.

"That ugly thing would look awful with this," I objected.

"Then take your umbrella," he said.

"Thanks. It's already in my car. Has Carter left for his game yet?"

"He's nonchalantly playing on his phone, but his bag's ready by the door, so I'm sure he's expecting his ride any time."

At that moment, we heard another car door. We glanced out and glimpsed an older-model, red Mustang leaving the curb. I briefly caught my son's profile in the passenger seat as it left. A different car pulled up, and I noticed the wipers swishing heavy raindrops off the windshield of Jackie's silver Lexus, as she parked where the boys had just been.

I ran down to open the door for Jackie, who hurried up the walk with her coat tented over her head. "Sorry," she said, "it's getting bad out there, and the traffic is terrible. We need to hurry."

As I gave Karl and my ten-year-old daughter, Sophie, kisses on our way to the garage, I said, "You'd better get going soon, too, or you'll miss the tip off. Enjoy the game, and take some video of Carter playing for me!"

Having passed two parking structures near the concert hall with bright-red, *Full* neon signs mocking us, I finally entered one about six blocks down, but drove around three floors before finding an open space. Neglecting to turn into it, I explained, "It's not safe to park in such a dark corner."

"No way, Lizzie! There are two of us, and we've got phones with flashlights. I can't miss the beginning of Ashley's show. We already have to walk several blocks in windy rain, so you'd better go back to that spot, or find another one pronto."

"I think I see one up there," I said, grumpily as it was more darkly isolated than the last, "and thanks for reminding me we need my umbrella. Can you please grab it from behind my seat?"

She reached back, and lifted up Sophie's small rainbow-polka-dotted one, with the curved purple handle.

"No," I said. "Mine's shorter. Feel around for a travel-sized one."

"There's nothing else back here."

"Let me check. I'd feel awful using Sophie's."

"Lizzie," Jackie admonished, with a warning tone, "this one's good enough. Let's go!"

I surreptitiously felt under my seat, and glanced around the back area as I got out and locked up, but quickly followed my sister, both to avoid more rebuffs, and to ensure I'd get under Sophie's umbrella before she left the covered area.

Jackie moved fast, being both more at ease in heels, and more motivated to find the auditorium. I held onto the shaft of the umbrella with her, trying to keep up, and was relieved to arrive at the glowing marquee with only some dampness on my black, angora coat sleeve.

"We still need the tickets from Will Call, don't we?" I asked, lowering the umbrella as she let go.

"Why don't you get them, while I get in line?" Jackie called, bolting toward the entrance, not waiting for me to question how she'd get in sooner, when Will Call bore the long line.

When I got to the window, the attendant discombobulated me by asking for my identification. I had to rummage through my purse, so nervous that the sympathetic man made polite small talk about the darkness of the storm's arrival, as he waited. I tried to smile through my discomfiture, and in gratitude for his calm understanding, after thanking him for the tickets, I commented on his lovely accent.

"You are kind," he answered. "I am new here from Nigeria."

By the time I caught up to Jackie, she appeared to be fidget dancing. She virtually dragged me to our seats, and we settled in as the curtain rose. I enjoyed the performance, but continued to jitter, presumably from the stress of getting there. What I appreciated most was watching Jackie's delight at witnessing her best friend Ashley's cello solo.

Luckily, her spotlight piece had ended before we heard a commotion behind us. Once we located the source of the disturbance, all we saw were the backsides of two ushers, who seemed to be carrying something, disappearing beyond the door to the lobby. It suddenly occurred to me that my subconscious had been nagging me to check around my feet for Sophie's umbrella. Nothing. I'd left it at Will Call!

The moment the lights went up for Intermission, I told Jackie, and headed back to retrieve it.

"That's the one Geemaw gave her on her ninth birthday, isn't it?" she asked.

"Yes, it's Grandma's last gift to her before she died. Sophie'll be devastated if I've lost it."

A different attendant sat behind the counter.

"I think I left a polka-dotted umbrella here."

"Sorry, haven't seen it," the woman said, as she smacked a wad of gum.

"Will you please ask the Nigerian man who was here before the show?"

"Akono? No, he's gone for the night. But you can check Lost and Found. It's inside on the left."

Back in the foyer, I received more attentive service, but could only fill out a Lost-Item report when they didn't have it either. I tried not to let my dejection dampen Jackie's enjoyment of the rest of the concert, but couldn't keep up the façade as the rain pelted us on our way back to the car. Attempting to protect my head with my coat, I exposed my back to the cold wet, and then marked the pinnacle of my misery with a broken heel, which caused my foot to slide off the curb into a frigid puddle.

I threw the flapping shoe across the intersection, stewing and grumbling, until I noticed Jackie quicken her steps to grab it off the street before a car could squash it. The way she cuddled it next to her body, as if she'd rescued a kitten, elicited a giggle from my throat, surprising me. She swung around, and after the initial shock of me taking off my other shoe to persist barefooted, she started to laugh, too. We were simply sisters, young again, frolicking in the downpour.

Sneaking into the house, stifling chortles like past-curfew teenagers, I noticed the TV room light still on. Karl gawked at my bare feet, but only shook his head and pointed at the television, saying, "Strangest thing. I'd never seen another umbrella like Sophie's until tonight, but the Mayor's on the news, explaining how a man shielded him from tonight's deluge with that one, as he escorted him into Emergency."

I stared at the screen, announcing, "That's Akono," at the exact moment Jackie asked, "Why's the Mayor in Emergency?"

"He slipped on the slick pavement and twisted his ankle as he arrived to visit his sister. She was hospitalized for a heart attack she suffered while at your concert. Lizzie, who's Akono?"

"That man there, holding Sophie's umbrella. I left it at his ticket counter by accident. Why'd he steal it? He seemed so nice."

"Calm down, sweetheart. We'll figure it out tomorrow."

Approaching home the next afternoon, I fumed. I'd been called to work early, and I'd had no time to check with the concert hall, hospital or TV station for explanations. When I walked in, Carter handed me the house phone.

"Mom, this lady wants to talk to you."

The reporter requested permission to interview us for her follow-up, umbrella-sharing story. After Akono had unexpectedly found and used it to shield the Mayor's sister, then the Mayor, and seventeen other people in and out of the hospital during the storm, he'd sought my identity, finding the Lost-Item report.

As I hung up, Carter said, "Sophie had to borrow someone's umbrella today, and now has a new friend. Oh, and I grabbed yours before I left last night. Thanks. My friend's aunt was at the game, and when we walked out to the parking lot, they were glad I had it, too."

I guess things aren't always what we choose to think.

FULL MOON

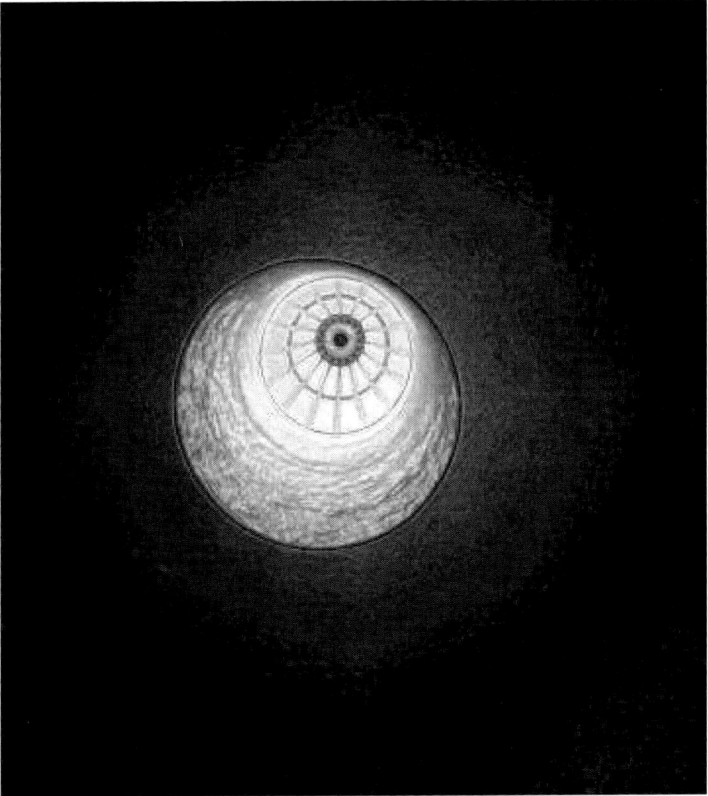

My Moon photographed by Carolyn Adams

CAT ON THE MOON by Jean Harkin

"There are nights when the wolves are silent and only the moon howls," wrote George Carlin in *Brain Droppings*. But this night was different. The moon was meowing—yowling and caterwauling—making a hullabaloo. Of course, I heard it—the whole neighborhood must have!

Stepping out to my deck from the night kitchen, I clearly saw a cat in the newly risen full moon. The silvery orb of reflected sunlight held the silhouette of a cat perched on the delicate limb of a tree. I contemplated this unearthly vision for several seconds, blinked my eyes, and then realized I was seeing a cat (probably mine) trapped on an outlying high branch of our dogwood tree. The full moon had situated itself perfectly to frame this cat-in-tree mirage.

Glad I wasn't hallucinating, I set my mind to figuring out what next— how to rescue my cat, Xena. She was facing the moon and crying out in her loudest Xena voice. Momentarily, I wondered if she were trying to communicate with our neighboring world, maybe rejoicing in its shining glory. I watched and tried to assess her disposition. As her song of praise grew ragged and forlorn, I called her name softly so as not to surprise her.

Xena turned her white face toward me and let me know she was frantic, not moonstruck. She began batting a paw toward me, which caught her slightly off-balance. Grabbing with her paw, she regained position as the limb bounced. More pathetic vocalization from my truly stranded cat, and I felt her desperation. What to do! The branch she had climbed was too high for me to reach. I quickly dismissed the derring-do of standing on the deck railing to access the limb. It would still be too high. I thought of shaking the tree from a lower level, but I knew that would frighten Xena and probably make her hold tighter.

What were the options? Call for help from my computer-engaged husband Jack and have him set up a ladder in the dark to reach Xena? I imagined him suffering a bad fall. Phone 911? Or non-emergency rescue? First responders would definitely know what to do, having rescued stranded animals many times, at least on television!

Xena kept up her commotion and reminded me of her "I'm really, really hungry" pleadings. It was then an idea struck! I returned to the kitchen and walked past the clunking, churning dishwasher to where the electric can opener sat, unplugged it, and transferred it to the outlet near the open patio door. I engaged the can opener's whirring power and held my breath, watching Xena in the sky.

At a pause between her squalls, Xena turned her head to the sound of the can opener. Did she listen? Did she flick her ears? I thought so. I kept pressing on the can opener arm and let it whine into the night, hoping this familiar noise would distract my cat from fear and tempt her with anticipation of her favorite canned tuna entrée.

Like magic, the plan worked! Xena tenderly, timidly began to retreat backward down the spindly limb she'd climbed. Carefully, slowly she arched and twisted and tiptoed down to a sturdier branch, then jumped to the ground and hustled up the stairs to the open door where I stood in the kitchen. One look at her wide, sorrowful green eyes said it all—betrayal! She mewled, "Where's my tuna?" and began pacing, voicing more hunger yowls.

I laughed and reached down to smooth her prickling fur. "You're okay now. And, of course, you shall have your feast."

Xena circled my feet as I loaded the odorous tuna delight into her blue and white kitty dish with the mouse painted at the bottom. "Watch your tail—I'll step on you!" As soon as I set the choice delicacy before her on the floor, I could see that Xena was *over the moon* with contentment.

Purrington's cat photographed by Jean Harkin

A YELLOW MOON ROSE by Carolyn Adams

A yellow moon rose
as the midnight fog lifted
to sleep in the trees

Montana Moon photographed by Louise Young

FIRST STEPS ON THE MOON by Jessie Collins

I am looking back to July 20th, 1969, when Neil Armstrong and Buzz Aldrin reached the climax of their epic journey. How well I remember that amazing day when we watched in awe as those two young men landed in their spaceship on the Moon, and then took their first steps onto that strange soil.

I was an elementary school teacher in a small school in England. We had an infants' department containing two classes and a junior department with three classes, and the staff comprised of headmaster, deputy head, and three other teachers. One would have thought that so small a number of adults might be in agreement about the importance—or otherwise—of the television broadcast of this momentous happening, but one would have been wrong. Neither the headmaster nor the deputy head thought it worthwhile to cancel normal lessons and watch the broadcast. The young lady who taught the lowest junior class (ages 7/8) thought it would be worth watching, but the headmaster decided that her class was too young to gain anything from this. The middle junior class (ages 8/10) was taught by me, and the other member of staff who wanted the children to see history being made was the lady who taught the top juniors (ages 10/11). We two were told "Very well. Go ahead if you feel you must. Put your two classes together in the TV room."

We spoke to the children in our classes about the importance of the program we were about to watch, and how we hoped that they would remember in future years what they had seen and be glad that they had had the opportunity to see it. Then the broadcast began. There were little murmurs of excitement from time to time, but the behavior of those children in that crowded room was remarkably good, for they were all showing real interest in all that was happening. Discussion afterward brought some intelligent observations and questions, and in the time-honored fashion of those school days we had the children write in their notebooks about what they had seen.

A number of years later I happened to meet up with one of those children—now a young woman. We chatted, and she said how glad she and her friends had been to be allowed to watch those first steps on the Moon, and how they had enjoyed being able to talk with others about it. I really felt justified that two of us on the staff of that small school had cared enough about the making of history to want those children to share in it.

THE SERENADE OF A FULL MOON by Susan Apurado

Listening to the sob of the waves
Under the golden shimmering sky
Brings back sweet childhood mem'ries
We sourly left behind

With you in each moment
There's a summer in my soul
With you in each moment
My world is fragrant and gentle

We used to laugh or simply cry
We used to compete or fiercely fight
To the countless piffle things
And petty games like flying a kite

Those days were just a blink of an eye
As we turned the pages of our lives
We no longer raced like enemies
But as a team lavish of starlight dreams

I threw a stone into the sea
You whispered it with a wish
That someday on this life's journey
We would share a lifelong dish

As we wrapped in each other's arms
The music played in a celestial tune
As we looked up the beaming skies above
Our hearts danced to the serenade of a full
moon...

Painting by
Susan Apurado

THE WOLVES by Matthew McAyeal

A long time ago, in the twilight before a night of the full moon, a young Puritan colonist named Constant Turner was barricading himself into his home. This was not an unusual activity at the moment, as all the townspeople were doing the same. The difference was that they were hoping to keep danger out while Constant was hoping to keep danger in.

It was thus a most inopportune time for someone to knock on his door. A knock came nonetheless.

"Go away!" he barked.

"Please, Constant!" said a very sweet voice. "I need your help!"

The voice belonged to Obedience Child, the local seamstress and the prettiest of seven nubile sisters. Her sisters were named Patience, Mercy, Thankful, Hope, Unity, and Rachel. Constant had gotten to know Obedience quite well recently, since he needed so much clothing repaired these days.

"Find someone else!" he said. "I cannot help you right now!"

"Constant, please!" she begged. "It has to be you and it has to be right now!"

He couldn't say no to Obedience for long. Against his better judgment, he let her in. He knew he'd have to get her to leave before the darkness came, but how long could this take?

The familiar sight of Obedience's beauty was revealed as she stepped inside—her fresh face, fair skin, dark hazel eyes, and the little curl of dark hair peeking out from under her white coif. Like all the townswomen, she wore simple Puritan garments, but Constant did not think that the robes of a queen could have enhanced her beauty. Surely even Louis XIV, in his decadent court across the sea, could not hope for a woman so beautiful!

Constant knew her well enough to know that her beauty on the outside was matched by beauty on the inside. She was not only a God-fearing hard worker, as any good Puritan colonist would be, but friendly, helpful, and cheerful. She always smiled a most loving smile at her fellow creations. Even now she was smiling, only it was a bit more nervously than normal. Constant hoped she would always smile at him like that, but her smile would disappear really quickly if she stayed there much longer…

"Constant, I need your help," she said. "My father wants me to marry John Black."

"Do you want to marry him?" asked Constant, trying to keep his voice even. He hated John Black and was sickened by the thought of Obedience marrying him, but Constant wasn't exactly in a position to pass moral judgment on anyone else.

"No," said Obedience. "I cannot marry him. He is a wicked, ungodly man! You remember what he did to that Indian village during the war. That was the same night the wolf attacks started. It is God's judgment against us, I am sure of it! But you knew it was wrong at the time. That's why you stayed behind with the men building the palisade."

"Yeah, I suppose I did," said Constant awkwardly. "Maybe you should go now."

"It's dreadfully ironic that you were the first victim of the wolf attacks and on that very night no less," she continued. "As I recall, you found yourself naked in the forest when you woke up the next morning. I still don't understand how that happened. And just a month later, your entire family were the wolves' next victims. Oh, Constant! I feel so bad for you and so afraid as well! How do the wolves get past the palisade?"

"Well, no one knows that," Constant lied. "You should go now."

"Constant, I want you to marry me!" Obedience declared. "Believe me, I know my father wouldn't be happy with the match, but I don't care! You're the only godly choice! I'm ready to give up everything for the Lord and I can only do that with you!"

"No, you can't," said a gruff voice suddenly.

At that moment, John Black himself burst in the door. He was a tall, handsome man with shining black hair and he was pointing a musket at Constant!

"If you think this is the way to court me, you are wrong!" Obedience yelled indignantly.

"I'm not doing this to win your favor, woman," John said with a condescending sneer. "I'm saving the town for a second time."

"You didn't save it the first time!"

"I did what I had to do," he drawled. "Why should I have spared their women and children? The children would only grow up and the women would only breed more of them. My only regret about the war is that I didn't kill King Philip myself!"

"And how are you saving the town now?" asked Obedience, crossing her arms.

"By putting an end to *his* attacks!"

"Wolves are behind the attacks!"

"No," said John, shaking his head. "One wolf is. Him. He's a werewolf, Obedience! The attacks always come during the full moon, the same nights he's always too ill for his militia duties. But it's over now. The silver bullet I've loaded into my musket will see to that!"

"Werewolves!" scoffed Obedience. "Surely that's an old pagan myth! We Puritans know better than to believe such foolish superstitions!"

But even as she spoke those words, thick hair had started bursting out all over Constant's body. "Go! Go!" he yelled at Obedience. "Get out of here!"

"I will not leave with John Black!" she declared proudly.

"He's right about me!" yelled Constant, speaking quickly while he still could speak. "The wolf which attacked me was a werewolf and I became one when I was bitten! The next time I changed, I killed my own family! I'll kill you next if you don't leave! I've tried to stop the attacks, but the beast always finds a way! I couldn't tell anyone! I didn't want anyone to know! I really, really didn't want you to know because I—because I love y—" At this point, the growth of huge wolf fangs suddenly made him incapable of human speech.

Constant hated the way Obedience was looking at him now—with big, fearful eyes and not even the slightest smile. She was scared—scared of *him*! And she ought to be too, since the beast was rising up within him and he could already feel its monstrous impulse to rip apart her vulnerable, delicate body. Oh, how he wished he could save her from the danger! That would bring back her beautiful smile for sure! But he couldn't. He *was* the danger.

He flailed and snarled as he came down on all fours and burst out of his clothes. He was not a person anymore. He was a beast now. He did not recognize Obedience as a special person or even a person at all. She was just something to kill in the hopes that it would help satiate his violent fury. His only concern was that she wouldn't be enough—not even close to enough! He would have to kill a lot more people than just her, so he'd better get started!

The werewolf lunged forward.

Obedience screamed in terror.

John fired his weapon.

The silver bullet found its mark.

Tension dissipated as the werewolf collapsed. Being dead, Constant was spared the sight of Obedience collapsing romantically into the arms of her rescuer, John Black.

DUSKING ON A LONE COAST by Carolyn Adams

The moon, a sad
wanderer, stakes claim
to a mirror-lake,
while I wonder
where you are.
Are you also lost
in yourself, lost
in sorrow, lost
to the world?
Do you watch the darkness
gather, counting the hours
before you rise again
with the sun,
to plot a course
that leads only
to another deep
and silent night?

Full Moon photographed by Louise Young

FREEZE, FLEE OR FIGHT by David Lutes

My name is Moon—but not the moon in the sky. Moon is a Burmese name with an ancient history. I'm 36 years old now but I want to tell you what happened when I was a child. Our family moved to New York City from Burma (now called Myanmar) before I was born. The Burmese Minister of Foreign Relations had appointed my father to Chief of Staff of the Burmese delegation to the United Nations. I was born in New York but didn't receive US citizenship because of my father's diplomatic status.

When I was twelve years old the political situation in Burma went through a violent change. My father came home from the UN and told us that the new Minister of Foreign Affairs had fired the Ambassador to the US and ordered the UN staff to return to Burma. I didn't really understand what had happened but we packed our belongings and flew from Kennedy Airport to Tokyo. We were scheduled to transfer to a flight to Rangoon but Dad mysteriously phoned some associates and announced we would stay in Japan for a day or two. Little did I realize that I would remain in Tokyo for three months.

We stayed in an apartment for several days and then Dad announced he was flying alone to Rangoon (now Naypyidaw). He wanted to leave Mom and me in Tokyo until he either sent for us or returned to Tokyo. Mom insisted that she go with Dad, and they left me in the hotel with Yumi, a Japanese lady who worked at the US Embassy in Tokyo. The next morning Yumi came to our hotel.

"Ohayo Gozaimasu," she said as she sat down to talk to Dad and Mom. I went to my room but stood by the door and listened to their conversation.

Dad began. "I am very worried. We need to return to Burma but, as you know, the situation there is out of control and quite dangerous. So we don't want to take Moon with us."

"I understand," replied Yumi. "At the Burmese Embassy some people are refusing to leave and, Mr. Moon, some on the staff say you shouldn't go. You could be sent to prison or…"

"I realize the risk but I must return for personal reasons. I plan to help my wife's sister and her husband leave Burma. We expect to return here in one week."

As I listened to the conversation I started to feel afraid. I sat on the edge of my bed, my body frozen, stressed and tense. The next day Mom and Dad flew off to Rangoon.

Several weeks dragged by and the next thing I remember was Yumi telling me that her friend, somebody named Pat, was coming to visit us. Later in the day Pat, an American man, came to our room and sat down across from Yumi and me. He was wearing a suit and his bald head shined like it had oil on it. He shook hands with Yumi and I noticed he was paying considerable attention to me. He wasn't smiling. I could tell from the way he spoke to Yumi that he understood business at the Embassy and was probably a high ranking member of the staff—like my father had been. He seemed very serious and spoke in a soft voice like he didn't want to frighten me.

"Moon, I work with some people in Rangoon and they have informed me that your father and mother arrived a few weeks ago."

I felt fear because of his seriousness. Then I looked at Yumi and saw tears coming to her eyes as she placed her arms around me.

"Yesterday we learned, Moon, that the Army arrested your father, took him to a building near the Army base, and now we have received word that he has died."

At first I didn't understood what Pat said. Yumi's tears started running down her cheeks. I started to cry a little but everything seemed so dreadful. As we sat there Pat put his hand on my shoulder.

"Please understand, Moon, I am here to help you. We can work things out. But for now, I'm sad for you and I'll do everything I can to make things better."

I just sat there and then as I started to understand I asked, "Is my mother okay?"

"We don't know, Moon. We are working to find out but we haven't seen her."

***

That night I didn't sleep. I didn't move. I realized that everything in my life had disappeared. I had no home, my dad and mom were gone, and I had nothing connecting me to the world I had known. I looked around. Everything felt foreign. I felt unconnected with everyone and I didn't think anyone wanted me. As my fear grew I sensed my life had ended. I just closed down. I didn't think, I didn't feel, and I barely moved.

Pat came back the next day to talk but I hid in my room. He spoke to Yumi for a few minutes and then left. I felt like a tiny mouse with a cat coming closer and about to pounce.

Pat continued to visit. I learned much later that he had contacted the Japanese government, the UN, and US Immigration. The good news: The Japanese government would not deport me to Burma/Myanmar given the political situation. However, should I leave Japan, I wouldn't qualify for a visa to return. As for the US, I was not a US citizen and thus had no basis for residence in the US. When Pat started visiting, I was afraid to talk to him or even look at him. I didn't leave my room. I heard Pat tell Yumi to take me to a doctor but I didn't want to go. I just sat there.

Several days later Pat and Yumi took me to a school where kids my age were playing. One came over and greeted us. He looked at me and we both smiled.

"Let's play dodgeball—you can be on my team!" Four or five other boys joined us and pointed ten yards away to another team. "They have the ball and they throw first."

The other team started running toward us. One of the players picked up the ball and looked directly at me. Then he lifted his arm and threw the ball. I still remember the ball hitting me hard in my stomach. I stood there and all of a sudden I felt something inside me explode. I screamed and cried, ripped off my shirt and started running, I couldn't take it anymore. I tried to flee the playground and run away forever. Pat grabbed me, threw me over his shoulder as I kicked and screamed, and carried me to the edge of the field. Every emotion poured through me. I couldn't stop crying. Pat hugged me and when my exhaustion took over he looked directly into my eyes and started to talk.

"Moon, you will be okay. You are not alone. You are safe. I feel bad for all that has happened but let's talk about what we want to do." I just stood there frozen. "You must fight to get what you want. Pretend you are near a light switch. If you have fear, the light switch is off. You just want to sit in your room or run away. If you turn the switch on, it gives you courage to fight. Can you do that?" I understood and nodded.

"Moon, Flip the switch!" He took my hand in his, reached outward and guided me through the motion of flipping the switch. Something began to change within me and I started to speak to him bravely for the first time.

"Yeah, I can do 'flip the switch' but I want to go back to my school in New York. I want to go home." I started crying again but this crying was different. Saying I wanted to go back to America gave me a dream for my life and a purpose.

Pat squeezed my hand, "Let's do what we have to do to take you home. I know we can do it. But, just remember the switch. When you have darkness and fear just 'Flip the Switch' and drive your fears away."

I didn't know then but the next day Pat returned to America. He visited New York and talked to my school principal and arranged for me to return to my old class. Then he started searching for a home in the same neighborhood where I had lived with Mom and Dad. He also learned that Japan would let me exit but wouldn't issue a visa to return. America wouldn't permit me to enter and Burma had cancelled my passport. So, Pat made a plan. First, Pat would arrange a "job" for me on a Philippine freighter stopping in Japan and then sailing on to San Francisco. If people asked me, I was to become a deckhand on the ship. When I reached San Francisco somebody would meet me. After that, Pat said, I would be fine but he didn't tell me anything more. I promised to stick to his plan.

Just before I left Japan, Pat brought me some clothes—they had the name of "Aquino Freight Lines" on them—and he and Yumi drove me to a huge freighter in the port of Yokohama. Seeing the ship and knowing I'd be on the ocean with no one I knew made me afraid. I began to sweat—maybe it was the hot day or was it my fear starting to build. Pat and Yumi gave me a hug and as I started up the ladder to the main deck, they both waved. I was on my own. I stood there and my fear started to return. I froze and then remembered the switch. I reached out my hand and flipped it. I looked around, waved back to Yumi and Pat and boarded the ship.

My trip, sad to say, wasn't much fun. Although I thought I was going to work, the crew had nothing for me to do and I lay in my bunk most of the time or leaned over the starboard side vomiting because I was seasick.

Several days later we tied up at the Port of San Francisco. Some workers came aboard to operate cranes to unload the ship. Then a tall man came aboard and asked for me. I met him on the quarterdeck.

"Hi. Welcome to America."

"I am Moon," I said with some hesitation.

"Hello, Moon, I'm a friend of Pat—you know Pat?"

"Sure, he's in Japan."

"Well," the tall man began, "what does Pat always say when he's scared?"

"Flip the Switch," I answered.

"You got it!"

The tall man then told me that I was about to start a three-day vacation. He drove me to a ranch where I relaxed and had fun riding a horse. I thought it strange to vacation on a ranch but I was so happy to get off the ship and walk on land.

After three days the tall man drove me back to San Francisco. I thought we were going back to the freighter but he told me the freighter had already left port for the Philippines. Then he continued driving to an office. On the office door was a sign that read "Department of Immigration." At this point I had no idea what was happening. But, I had flipped the switch and realized I still trusted Pat's plan.

I sat down in the office and waited a few minutes. Then a lady stood in front of me. She wore a blue uniform and looked like a policeman.

"Are you Moon?"

"Yes, I am."

"Come with me." She led me to another room where she told me to touch a pad that recorded my fingerprints.

"Why are you doing this?" I asked. I felt like a criminal.

"You have entered the US illegally. We have been investigating you." I froze but remembered the switch. I felt like running away.

Then, the lady took me to an office. As soon as I walked in I experienced one of the biggest surprises of my life. An Immigration Officer sat at a desk and nearby stood Pat with a big smile on his face.

"Oh, Pat! We did it!" I yelled.

Pat rushed over, bumped my chest—like football players do when they score a touchdown.

"You did it!" he yelled.

"I'm back in America." Tears flowed from my eyes.

A few moments later the Immigration Officer began to speak. He ordered me to sit down near his desk.

"Moon, you have entered the US illegally. Also, I must inform you that if you say anything it can be used… oh, just don't say anything." I nodded.

"First, I have received a copy of a document from the UN that designates you a political refugee. You have Burmese citizenship but you can't prove it and have no passport. You are also a minor whose parents are no longer available to take care of you. We would send you back but we don't know where 'back' is. So, the US proposes to handle your illegal entry in the following way. First, we recognize your refugee status. Accordingly, we grant you asylum in the US and can issue you a permanent residence card. Additionally, we can issue you a special US passport to use for identification and travel. Finally, you have been legally emancipated and Pat has made arrangements for you to attend school in New York and live with a family in your old neighborhood. If you agree with these conditions, sign here."

I picked up a pen, looked at the paper and looked toward Pat. I was shocked. He no longer stood there and had left the room. Here I was, alone on my own. I had lost everything and then suddenly realized I was no longer a child but was becoming a man. I was also becoming an American. I had fought for my dream and I won. I was beginning a new life. I signed the paper.

Thanks to Pat, I had "Flipped the Switch!"

***

I moved back to New York, graduated from high school and then went to university in California. I met Brenda. We married and have two kids. Thankfully, we live in new times. Several years ago President Obama visited Burma and soon I hope to travel there, find out what happened to my mother and visit my father's grave. I feel some fear when I think of going to a country where I lost my family but now I know how to use my fear to make my life better.

Based on the story of a Burmese person assigned to the UN whose son had a number of citizenship issues when the father was recalled after a change of government in Burma. The Burmese Embassy withheld the son's passport and he ended up in Japan. While this story has some fictional elements, the author did personally meet the son

WATER, WATER EVERYWHERE

Behind Upper Horsetail Falls photographed by Carolyn Adams

MIRAGE by Karen Alexander-Brown

With what seemed to be her last ounce of strength, Malika lifted the edge of her shawl that served as a tent against the relentless heat of the sun. Flashes of intensified light reflected off the water that surrounded the makeshift raft and instantly blinded her. In reflex her free hand flew to shield her squinting eyes. The brusque action jostled the limp body of her infant daughter in her sling near Malika's breast.

Had she heard a weak voice from around her say, "Look there"?

Other sweaty bodies pressed in against hers and Malika's hand returned protectively to the child. It had been a couple of days since the constant cries of hunger from her daughter had lulled the child into long bouts of fitful torpor. Malika's own gnawing hunger pains had subsided into a constant dull ache. Her salt-caked feet were dry, flaking and splitting from constant contact with the water and bodily fluids in the bottom of the raft. The increasing stench turned her stomach, but there was nothing to retch up from her shriveled stomach. She had little or no milk in her breasts to feed her child.

All eyes were on the horizon as the glorified raft lifted and sank with the rise and fall of the glinting dark water all around them. There had been many false alarms before, so everyone tried to focus weak eyes outward in a suspended silence.

What appeared to be a jagged ribbon of land bobbed in and out of sight on the horizon with the up and down motion of the raft. Slowly a speck appeared, moving toward them. As the racing boat moved closer into view, shouts rang out from the raft and the refugees waved ragged pieces of clothing in the air. Malika cried tears of exhaustion and relief.

By the time the boat reached the raft, the celebration had subsided and the refugees all stood in tense anticipation of their uncertain fate. The sailors, possibly Coast Guard, were shouting orders in Italian. Few, if any, of the refugees understood what they were saying, but they followed the actions as best they could, catching cast out ropes and hanging on.

Wrapped modestly in her shawl and hugging her human cargo, Malika was one of the first to be helped off the unwieldy raft. She politely averted any direct gaze, but in her exuberant gratitude, she grabbed and kissed the hand of one of her rescuers, mumbling in her own language, "Thank you! Thank you! May you be blessed."

Now they were the human cargo of the Italians and at their mercy. Surely it could not be worse that the certain horrible deaths they faced in their war-torn lands?

Photograph by Karen Alexander-Brown

JETSAM by Sheila Deeth

Summer tide spinning my soul to your side
Flotsam all jettisoned, weed-tangled shrine
Freed from the ocean to die, left behind.

Cape Meares photographed by Carolyn Adams

SPLASHES OF CHILDHOOD by Judy Beaston

Our home could be a mausoleum of silence now the boys live in their own homes. But echoes of their presence reach my ears from every room. One of my favorites is the bathroom where untold baths covered walls and floors with water, soapy water.

One year, Greg and Henry went through a phase of warships and ocean battles. Henry, the oldest of our boys, led the way and Greg, next in line, followed him like a shadow.

In everything, what Henry played, Greg played. When Henry biked through the park, Greg rode his bike, sans pedals, feet powering him along. And when Henry decided he would be the captain of a huge war vessel when he grew up, of course Greg was by his side, dreaming naval dreams.

They accumulated boats in many sizes, thanks in part to a generous grandfather who was a retired navy captain. The boys' water battles filled—or flooded—one entire summer before Henry changed allegiances. But during that summer, I was surrounded by water, water, everywhere!

The bathroom, of course, but tubs were used in the kitchen when thunderstorms halted outdoor play. Backyard play kept the water outside but often led to muddy spots and puddles. One day, the patio flooded when Greg left the water running. Lucky for us, our patio is one step down from the back entry or I would have needed a boat to navigate my kitchen.

In the heat of August that year, we stayed for a week at a lake in Wisconsin. At last the boys could be real captains on real boats—with Dad along as a boatswain's mate, of course.

That was the first of many summers on the lake, though the only one with both boys playing navy games. High school, girls, college all seemed to follow in fast succession.

Henry left military dreams behind for botany, Brenda and their home on Lake Michigan. He still captains a boat, but his life rides quieter waters than those of his childhood.

Greg, however, never lost that big boat seed. It grew and blossomed, much to his grandfather's delight. That's where he is today, on a huge navy vessel, ready for warrior action, should it be needed.

His wife and one-year-old twin sons wait at home. I'm going over there today, to enjoy a summer afternoon with them. There will be a little pool in the backyard, of course. I think I'll bring one of Greg's old warships for the boys. And a change of clothes in case the battles get fierce.

WATER, A MYSTERY... by Susan Apurado

Water, water, everywhere
I truly wonder
What's the mystery
Lies within

Water in the pond
With lilies and leaping frogs,
Toads and happy swans
All radiant under the sun

Water roars in the stony river
Pristine and crystal clear
It gets frozen in wintertime
It glitters in summertime

Waterfall streams gently
Onto the floor on earth's soil
Amazes every creature who'll see
Appreciating Creator's majesty

Water in the air, on the surface,
Below the ground and in the oceans
Fresh waters and frozen in glaciers
Where has it all strangely been?

Photograph by Susan Apurado

GENESIS by Carolyn Adams

Before memory,
something slow-moved
over water,
exquisite
in the way
that it moved.

Seas crested
in quivering
sheets,
whispering:
This mystery,
this single moment,
contains us.
Mist,
rainfall.
This is where we are going.

Lower Horsetail Falls photographed by Carolyn Adams

And so it was
that air and ocean
spoke,
in languages foreign to us,
the words
that dreamed us
into being.

UNDERCURRENT OF THE POND by Jean Harkin

Sunny reflections like shimmering diamonds reveal a swiftly-moving current through the bright cold water of Rood Bridge Pond. Teal ducks in green eye masks are swimming with their families and quacking at neighbors. A Canada goose family of three adults and a troupe of youngsters amble about on a grassy island near the opposite shore. With them is a white domestic goose, having found a friendly group of companions. A Steller's jay squawks and flits, flashing blue, through the trees above us. The musky scent of skunk cabbage rises from the damp mud.

Sue and I enjoy the peaceful morning scene as we stroll around toward the far end of the pond along a narrow path crowded with tree roots and small stones. We are curious to discover the source of the cruising current. I suggest, "Rock Creek probably flows through the pond there."

We arrive at the opposite shoreline only to discover the pool is completely enclosed by a bank that rises up at that end. "Hmm!" says Sue, shrugging her shoulders and looking puzzled.

"Odd, isn't it!" There is no apparent inlet to the pond. I can only guess that the moving water is caused by an underground spring. I share my theory, and Sue nods.

"Probably so," she says, biting her lip, frowning as if uncertain.

The sparkling current is one of those little mysteries that remind me how much of the natural world is unknown. But that is okay with me. I like that nature is more mysterious than familiar. The magic and mystery of nature feed our imaginations and lead us to new levels of awareness and knowledge.

The glittering rivulet plying its way through Rood Bridge Pond reminds me of the "river beneath the river" that Clarissa Estes refers to in *Women Who Run With the Wolves*. The sub-surface stream beckoning Sue and me at the little pond is like the stream of the collective unconscious that we step into when engaging the creative and spiritual aspects of the mind. Where do those inspired words, enlightened solutions, the *aha* moments of insight come from?

Moments of surprising inspiration when I'm focused on writing cause me to wonder how certain words or ideas flow from my own brain—like a treasure floating up from the depths of a stream I've bravely stepped into. Stream of consciousness? The currents within the soul and the underwater channel through the pond are miracles and gifts to accept and appreciate. Why question the sources? For me, these will remain mysterious and wonderful.

THE LAST TIME I SAW...

Landscape painted by Karen Alexander-Brown

AS IN IDENTICAL by Robin Layne

"The last time I saw my brother was twenty years ago. He didn't look so good."

Randy was amazed to hear the words flow from his own mouth. He closed his eyes, trying to block out both the mental intrusion from the female roadie before him and the images that bombarded his mind. It was too much to handle at once. The girl had asked him if he had a brother who looked anything like him.

"Why was it so long ago?" she pried. "Did something happen to him?"

The singer covered his face, barely aware that he was sitting on a speaker on the stage and roadies were helping his backup band pack up the equipment. "Please," he pleaded. "Leave me alone."

But she didn't. "There *is* another man as handsome and charming as you, who isn't chained to a wedding ring?"

"My twin is—"

"*Twin?*" she bubbled. "You have a twin? As in—*identical?*"

Randy inhaled briskly. Why her, of all people? This rude young fan had broken open his secret vault of memories, and now the memories occupied him so much he couldn't block her path into his mind. Generally, telepathy had to work both ways. Had he somehow opened himself to her?

"Mandolin Randolin!" she squealed, oblivious to his foul mood. "What's *his* name? Is he a musician, too? Where have you been hiding him?"

All Randy managed aloud was a groan. Where indeed was his brother? In a grave in his home country of Hoteree, in another dimension that he had been happy to escape. The naturally pale complexion both twins shared had looked hideous on Lord Randamir in the coffin—so white, so unlike the man he had been. Fortunately, Randolin, as the singer was called in his original home in Hoteree, had at least had the presence of mind to close his brother's eyes after the duel. But he couldn't erase those dead light-green eyes from his vivid inner sight. It was as if it were himself he had killed, and as if he could never truly be alive again.

"Randy?" He barely heard the girl say the casual American name he had adopted eleven years ago when by an amazing feat of magic he and his friend Brent had traded dimensions and countries. "*Randal!*" she tried when he didn't answer.

"Randolin" had become "Randal N.," and since he had played mandolin for almost as long as he could remember, the nickname "Mandolin Randolin" had developed here in the New World and helped catapult him to fame. None of that mattered to him at the moment.

"What's the matter?" The roadie waved her hands in front of his face, but it had no meaning for him. His brother lay before him, bleeding from several wounds. Randamir ("Amir" for short) had proved himself as hardy as he was cruel. Randolin won the fight only because Amir relied heavily on the raven demon who had helped him murder his family and his king and take over all Hoteree. In an unexpected moment, the captured queen had invited the demon to go attack her where she was imprisoned—an act of self-sacrifice for her country. But Randolin couldn't pause to find out if she, who had ordered him to kill his twin, lived. He had to complete this horrible task while the demon was away and unable to save Amir. Tears streaking his face and blurring his vision, he ran Amir through with the sword he had practically sold his soul to get. A sharp empathetic pain pierced his own heart; both brothers convulsed. Blood poured from Amir's chest and mouth. Both men screamed as one. Something talon-like pulled at him, trying to wrench his spirit from his body. For a moment he forgot who he was.

Then, suddenly, the strong telepathic link he had had with his twin all his life ended. Randolin collapsed and fell unconscious.

***

Someone was shaking him. He kicked and flailed his arms, certain Lord Randamir's soldiers had come to slay him.

"Randy," a voice buzzed in his ears. "It's okay. You're safe. Did you hurt yourself when you fell?"

"Make certain no one desecrates his grave," Randy murmured.

"What is he talking about?" said the roadie girl.

"It's an attack of PTSD," his backup flutist said. "War trauma. Don't try to make him talk about it. It's a torment he relives sometimes. This isn't the place or time to let that cat out of the bag."

Randy was grateful for the musician's support. He hoped the roadie hadn't realized she had tapped a place in his mind he normally kept buried... especially when he was on tour, which was most of the time lately. He refocused his eyes on her face. She appeared to be trying to show sympathy now, though it might be beyond her capability. With latent telepathic abilities, a person without sympathy could be dangerous indeed. That fact Randy knew too well. How had the one person identical to himself turned out to be a mass murderer?

Amir hadn't started out that way. He was once a wonderful childhood companion.

Randy swallowed the bile in his throat. He worried over what he was becoming himself. Amir had killed many in his impatient grab for power. All Randy had now he had gained in the New World: Patricia, his gentle, beautiful wife; and three five-year-old sons, identical triplets with strong pathing abilities like their father. He didn't like to admit that the main reason he stayed away from home so much of the time was to protect them—from himself. When he was near them, they picked up on his nightmares and flashbacks. It was far too much for a five-year-old to endure or understand, much less three of them feeding on one another's thoughts and emotions. Patricia tried to understand, but he knew she cried often out of loneliness and frustration. The nanny was no substitute for the man she loved. He was driving her into depression. He wouldn't blame her if she found solace in someone else's arms. As for him, too often the same audiences he led into his telepathic visions swept him into oblivion until, to his shame, he found himself doing things he had not intended—with people he should barely know, but who swiftly became intimate with him.

Was he any better than his brother? He wasn't sure… If he fought off their advances, he might hurt them, even kill again. Perhaps he really had lost his soul when he killed Amir. Or no—the loss was certain but gradual. He had to gain more love than his twin had ever known before he destroyed that love through neglect and abuse.

"We'll be waiting in the van!" the flutist called.

Randy barely heard. He looked up to see the auditorium empty and a single light left on to aid his departure.

Dueling Twins painted by Robin Layne

The account of Randolin's arrival in Portland from his original Hoteree, "Changing Planes," is in The Writers' Mill Journal Volume 5. *Find a younger Randamir earlier in this volume in "A Dark and Stormy Knight."*

TEDDY by Lauri Leonetti

"The last time I saw that teddy bear was twenty years ago. It didn't look so good." I frowned into the phone as I spoke, stopping myself from continuing out loud, *Yeah, ever since…* Then I quit thinking it, too. Pauline had surprised me during her account of her newest discoveries, and my response despaired more than I wanted to admit.

"It still doesn't," she answered, "but it's better than I would've expected."

"What do you mean?" I said caustically. "Do you think Mom fixed and cleaned it before stuffing it in that old attic trunk?"

I regretted my snarkiness, once the words spewed out of my mouth, but I was too affected to show contrition or take them back. I had too much ambivalence about her sorting through everything.

"Sorry, Andi," she said. "I just meant, after all these years, I expected it to fall apart more than it did. I shouldn't have said anything, but at least she stashed it, instead of destroying it like so many of our other treasures."

Now I felt horrible; she'd apologized and tried to be positive, when I'd been mean. But did she think I'd be excited about the resurrection of my souvenir of grief?

I tried speaking in a gentler tone, but couldn't dredge up any benevolent words yet. "It's not a treasure to me. It would've been better if she'd burned it."

"Come on, Andi," she pleaded, "from as early as I remember, you carried it everywhere, usually adorably tucked in your sweatshirt hood, so I don't know what you're saying. But I don't want to fight with you; I'm sorry I made you feel bad."

"I need *your* forgiveness, Pauline. You called with something you thought I'd enjoy, right? I ruined your excitement. Let's not discuss your explorations at the house anymore. Anything new with the girls or Jeremy?"

"No. Nothing since last week's talk. What about you? When do you get time off with your latest job?"

"I'm still not eligible for three weeks. If Mom actually died, rather than going into an Alzheimer-care facility, I could take bereavement leave." I briefly paused, but knew I'd dug up another bone I'd better kick a bit of dirt back over, so I hurried on, "I'll start looking at flights tonight, and email you when I've made reservations."

"Thanks. I promise to box up all the bad-memory stuff, so you can stay in the house. There're still too many things needing to be done: repairs, interviewing realtors, bank and legal mumbo-jumbo, before we can put it on the market anyway."

Tempted to respond with wishing the house itself could be hidden in a box, I didn't want to upset her more. I'd known I couldn't sleep there alone in the dark, so I said, "Jenna's offered a room at their place. That'll make it easier to spend some time with her while I'm home."

"Oh, okay," Pauline replied, with an obviously-fake understanding tone, masking hurt. I knew to cut this call quickly, as nothing could improve it. I didn't expect her to lift the lid off the subject I'd just peeked into, and she especially surprised me with the genuineness of her attitude change.

"I actually understand, Andi. Jenna's your biological sister, too, so you connect in a significant way. She's safe to be around, since you haven't known her long enough to build up years of resentment. Also, I know how hard it is for me to be in Mom's proximity right now; I can only guess your issues after what happened between you and her. When you left, I figured out why you moved so far away. I'm fine if you want to sleep at Jenna's. Honestly." Then, before I responded, she hastily added, "Besides, you're saving me from the extra clean-up I was gonna do to ready the house."

As my plane touched down in Portland, I pondered why I wasn't landing on some tropical island, instead of using my few annual vacation days to visit my hometown of distressing memories and family, from whom I'd purposely distanced myself. Pauline, Angel and Missy flashed in my visual cortex, followed by Jenna, and I realized my stress teetered on only one family member. I'd been unfair to lump them all with her. I sincerely looked forward to seeing my sisters and the kids, and even my sisters' partners, but would have preferred altered circumstances. If only I made enough money to fly them all to vacation with me in Maryland.

On autopilot driving the rental car to Pauline's from the airport, I relived the wretched scene right before my senior prom. A few days before, Mom had perfunctorily consented to my wearing her gorgeous diamond and topaz necklace, which Pauline had worn to her prom a couple of years earlier. I'd selected a dress I knew it would complement beautifully. Nervous at her offhandedness, I'd hinted several times to assure she'd be home to open the safe when I needed it, but merely got brusque dismissals.

Deep in my cells, I sensed she didn't want me to borrow it, but more than simply annoying me—and it did, extremely—it confounded me. I imagined all kinds of scenarios to explain it, finally settling on one to appease my unrequited curiosity.

Since Pauline shared Mom's round face, fair hair, and slender build, but dark curls framed my longish features over my pear shape, I assumed that I must remind Mom of my father, whom I never knew. She never talked about him. Even though I asked, I never saw any photos, and Pauline didn't seem to know much more than me, only that he'd died before she'd turned three. When I was old enough to compute the math, I figured I'd been a few months old.

I envisioned a tragically sad event that took him from us, like an accident or a disease diagnosed too late, something that Mom didn't want to deal with, which would also give reason to her never having remarried, and scarcely dating. Perhaps the necklace came from him, and her grief prevented her from handling seeing it on me.

No matter what my imagination created, it didn't keep me from wanting the jewels to complete my outfit. As I'd suspected, she went 'out' that afternoon, and still hadn't returned half an hour before my date was to arrive. I panicked. I snuck into her room, angrily checked between her mattress and box spring, pulled everything from under her bed, rummaged through every drawer, every pocket in her clothes closet, every container on her wardrobe shelves, even every shoe, and every other place I could think that she might keep the key to the safe. I finally found it enclosed in a fake book on the shelf of her headboard.

I moved her hamper to get to the vault tucked behind it, between her dresser and the bed. As I pulled out the jewelry case, a packet of papers slipped out and scattered across the carpet. I picked up her Will first, but was quickly distracted from my nosiness about its contents when I spotted the word 'Adoption' on a folder that had slid partly under the bed.

My vibes of guilt and then alarm must have drawn her home. I heard the garage door open, and instead of stopping to hang her coat and use the bathroom, as she usually did when coming in, she came straight down the hall to fling her door wide, hitting me in the arm. I'd already seen enough, so I didn't feel the need to re-collect the documents once again strewn around me, as I huddled on the floor in my evening gown. My anguish and fury matched hers, and we were both too stubborn and wounded to listen to explanations, to forgive, or to answer the ringing of the doorbell which I had so anticipated earlier.

Pauline relayed the truth to me just before my graduation, at my friend Patsy's house, where I'd moved until I could finish school and leave it all behind. Mom admitted to her that I was right about being a disturbing reminder of my father. I looked like him, because I shared his genes, but the other half of me had come from an affair he'd had with a married woman. They had reconciled after his confessing and ending the dalliance, before I was born, but my biological mother's husband wasn't able to pardon her. After I arrived, his rage took hold, and he not only took her life, he hunted down my father as well.

Another folder from the safe, one I'd briefly perused, but hadn't understood, contained articles chronicling those events, the reasons my now-known-to-be-adoptive mother had never wanted to tell me about not sharing her blood. She'd acquiesced to the fact that no one else would take me. Since five-year-old Jenna went to her paternal grandparents, and my actual mother had no family available to claim me, Mom had begrudgingly adopted me.

The necklace, Pauline said, hadn't been our father's gift, but had belonged to our mom's grandmother, and she hadn't wanted me to get any ideas of claiming it. Of all this fresh knowledge, I couldn't exonerate the last fact, and it kept me from resolving things with her. I'd been an innocent, and I can't say I'd never felt loved—she must have softened after a while—so how could she treat me like that? I never would've expected her to give me that string of valuable gems, especially when I had an older sister, so why couldn't I have at least enjoyed them for one special night? Her crazed mix of jealousy, rejection and denial not only cost me the experience of my senior prom, but the stability of the one family I'd ever known.

Turning onto my sister's street brought me back to the reality that I hadn't spoken with the woman who'd always been my mom, in twenty years. Now, she had disappeared into the fogginess of her disease. I finally wanted to face her, but wondered if it could make any difference. Maybe I wanted to face her, because I knew it wouldn't make a difference. Maybe cowardice and fear controlled me, rather than the righteousness I'd clung to.

I fortuitously remembered a friend's recent words, while meeting for coffee to deliberate details of her reunion with her ex, that forgiveness has nothing to do with the person who offended you, but is actually a kindness you do for yourself, to reduce your attachment to the suffering the offense caused. I decided to be ready to forgive. No, I recognized I'd already forgiven her, and needed to see her.

After immediately indicating my intention to Pauline, I texted Jenna that I'd be later than planned, and we left for the care facility. Ten-year-old Angel joined us, and I appreciated the calming distraction and kindness.

"Aunt Andi," she said, "you forgot your jacket. My mom's old sweatshirt's back here. Wanna borrow it?"

Walking into the activity room, where Mom sat staring out the window, I suddenly felt six years old, wanting to pull the hood up over my head to hide.

"Don't expect much," Pauline whispered. "She hasn't recognized any of us in over three months."

I held my breath as the much smaller, non-intimidating version of the only parent I'd known looked up at me. No recognition.

I perceived Angel beside me, and momentarily caught sight of something brown and furry, as I felt her add weight to the hood hanging at my neck. While I touched the object and exclaimed, "Is that Teddy?" I heard Pauline admonish, "I told you to stay out of those boxes." Then, with a hopeful smile, Mom gasped, "Andrea? Is that you?"

First published in KICKSTART, an online writers' newsletter
by Nancy Woods

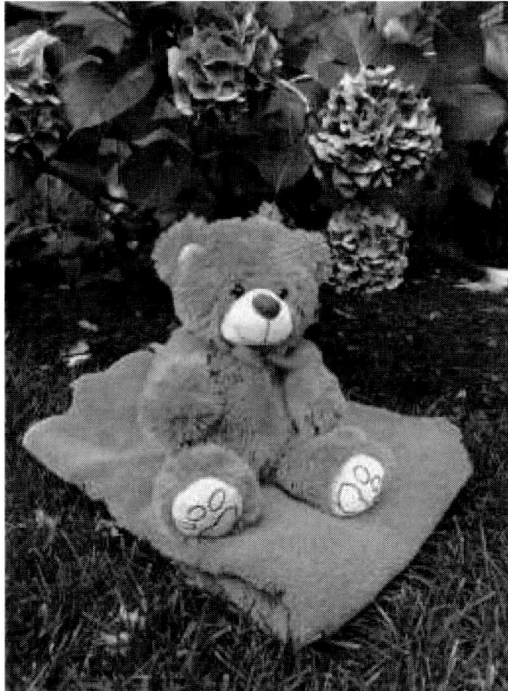

Teddy photographed by Judy Beaston

THE LAST TIME I SAW FLOWERS by Sheila Deeth

The last time I saw flowers was twen'y years ago. They didn' look so good. Kind o' scraggly, muted colors, dry as dust and sunburn. I 'member 'ow they clung to t' lee o' t' cliff, just edgin' out o' t' shadow for a couple hours a day. I used to stand 'ere lookin' up at 'em like they was jewels, little baby sunsets growin' out o' rocks. Then one day they was gone—not died, just all worn out and faded away.

So we've lived on tinned stuff since—it's all you've ever known, innit? Turnin' plastic handles; don't cut your 'ands on t' metal; watch out now; and Mommy, where do beans come from, and why are peas called green?

Come, walk with me. You 'member 'ow wet stuff fell out o' t' sky yes'erday? You asked me why t' sea was flying but it didn' taste right? Well, that was rain. And this is what 'appens after rain.

Up there, by that dark bit o' rock, on t' shadow's edge, canst see where I'm pointing? It looks like a baby sunset shinin' at you, dunnit? It's called a flower, my love, and we've survived.

Flowers photographed by Robin Layne

THE ARCHITECT by Karin Krafft

The last time I saw my brother was twenty years ago. He didn't look so good. In fact, he was face down outside our town's Irish pub, disheveled, his body oozing alcohol. Apparently he had handed someone a crumpled up piece of paper and sniveled, "Call my sister."

I got the call all right. Actually, I was more than surprised to get the call, as he was supposed to be in a rehabilitation center outside of town. I had planned to visit him the next day and he wasn't supposed to be out for at least two weeks.

"Hey Sis," he uttered as he saw me standing over him. That's what he always said when he wanted something from me. I was livid. I had cancelled my two-week holiday to Cancun with my boyfriend to pay for my brother's rehab. My wonderful boyfriend ended up going to Cancun by himself and that was the end of our relationship. I blamed it all on my brother, of course. Later I realized that the boyfriend was not such a nice guy after all.

My brother was seven years younger than I was and I had always protected him. Ever since he was born. He was my own living doll. I had lost count of how many times I had bailed him out of various precarious situations. I had covered for him and I had lied for him to our parents. I had paid for stolen alcohol, broken car windows, new clothes when he'd been in fights. Emptied my bank account. Now I'd had enough.

"You're dead to me," I said. "You're on your own. I never want to see you again. I mean it this time."

"Someone call the police," I said as I turned my back and walked away, trying to ignore his loud wailing. Covering up for him had taken over my life, and I couldn't take it anymore.

I never told our parents what had happened, but we never saw him again. l assumed he had run away and most probably died in a drunken stupor. I did think about him once in a while, but not often.

This particular morning, I had a splitting headache and had got an emergency appointment with my chiropractor to straighten out my back. Absentmindedly looking through a glossy magazine on the table, I gasped.

"American architect wins the prestigious Architect of the Year award for the third year in a row," in Melbourne, Australia. As I continued reading, I was flabbergasted. The man smiling into the camera was a ruggedly handsome middle aged man, with clear blue eyes and a healthy tan. His clothes looked expensive. A far cry from the long stringy hair and filthy clothes he was wearing that evening twenty years ago.

As I continued reading I forgot my splitting headache for a minute. How was this possible? My high school dropout of a brother, who never amounted to anything except getting in trouble and stealing from our parents, was an architect? And an award winning architect? The article said he had immigrated to Australia fifteen years ago after meeting the love of his life, an Australian woman visiting the United States. He was now an Australian citizen and enjoying life in Australia. Apparently he had no reason to return to the United States as he had no family left there. They were all dead. That hurt.

Why would he say that he had no family? He could easily have found me, if he had wanted to. I still lived in the same town we grew up in. Of course I could have found him too, but I never looked for him. I assumed he was dead. I burned with shame. What kind of sister was I? I should have looked for him!

My parents were no longer alive. They passed away believing that their son was a failure, and they never stopped blaming themselves. Had they been too old when they had him? What had they done wrong?

After my chiropractor's appointment, I called in sick for the rest of the day. There was no way I'd be able to get any work done. I went straight home and spent the next hours googling my brother. My gosh, was this person really my brother? He had won many prestigious awards over the years. I couldn't believe the photographs of his own home, one that he had designed of course. It was beautiful.

My mind was racing. Now that I had found him, what was I going to do about it? Obviously he had no interest in seeing me, or he would have tried. But then on the other side, I had told him that he was dead to me. And I had meant it; there was no doubt about that. I composed several messages on Facebook, but deleted them all. I didn't know what to say.

As soon as my seventeen-year-old daughter returned from school I had to explain to her that her long lost uncle, who was presumed dead, was not dead after all, but living the life in Australia. She had two cousins, a boy and a girl. I have to admit that I was afraid of her reaction, afraid that she would hate me for being a horrible person.

Instead, she surprised me. "I have cousins? In Australia? That's so cool. Let's go and visit them. School's out in two weeks, so let's start planning. Like now!"

I was torn whether I should write him or not, but we decided against it. If he didn't want to see me, I didn't want to know right away. Once we were physically in Australia, we'd contact him, and if he didn't want any contact, we'd have a nice vacation in Australia.

Two weeks later, my daughter and I landed in Melbourne, Australia, after a grueling long flight. Now that we were here, I was wondering if I was insane. What were we doing on the other side of the world?

"Mom, you think too much," my daughter said as she interrupted my thoughts. "Let's go and get the rental car."

Airport Scene photographed by Sheila Deeth

After checking into the hotel, we took a long nap, had dinner, and then went straight to bed. We had a big day ahead of us tomorrow.

The next morning the nice man at the reception desk explained in detail how to get to my brother's house. The closer we got, the more nervous I became.

"Oh my gosh Mom, there it is," my daughter exclaimed as the beautiful house appeared on the left side of the road. "It really is gorgeous, isn't it?"

I kept driving. What on earth had I been thinking? We couldn't just drop in like this. Could we?

"Mom, what are you doing? You passed it. You need to turn around. Look, right there, you can turn around here."

I was on autopilot now, and kept driving. My hands were shaking and my stomach was threatening upheaval.

"Mom, stop!"

My daughter's command woke me up and I stopped momentarily to catch my breath. "I'm okay now, really."

As I came to a stop in front of my brother's house, I saw a man coming out of the door with a black lab following close behind. Slowly, I got out of the car, grabbing my handbag for life support. As I approached him slowly, the lab was already there sniffing my shoes.

"Can I help you?" he started and looked straight at me.

Feeling paralyzed I couldn't get a word out; I just stared.

Suddenly, the familiar smirk appeared on his face and he said, "Hey Sis, I thought you never wanted to see me again."

Still frozen in my tracks, I must have looked like a complete moron, but I wasn't able to get a word out.

"It's not like you to be lost for words," he continued. "Come on in and meet the family. I assume this is my niece?"

"Come on Mom, move!" my daughter said as she marched behind her uncle into the house. "Let's meet my cousins."

"Yeah Sis, get a move on."

And just like that, twenty years evaporated and I had a brother again.

UNSPOKEN BONDS

Still Life With Lamp photographed by Carolyn Adams

ACROSS THE WALL by Matthew McAyeal

I was born the year they built the Wall. It was a hideous monstrosity of concrete, barbed wire, and guard towers. They said that the Wall was there to protect us, that the people on the other side were "fascists" and "revanchists." But everyone knew the truth. They didn't build the Wall to keep out dangerous enemies. They built it to keep us in.

Ever since I was a little girl, I felt drawn to a particular section of the Wall at a particular time of day. Every day that I could, I went to that part of the Wall at that time of the day and stood there, just for a minute or two. Of course, I had to be careful not to get too close to the Wall or else I'd be shot by the border guards who were there to "protect" us.

"What do you stand there for, Comrade Heidi?" I was sometimes asked.

"I don't know," I could only reply.

I couldn't explain it. I just had this vague feeling that there was something on the direct opposite side of the Wall calling to me. It was like I was meant to be joined to it, but was cut off instead. Even if I could have explained this feeling, I wouldn't have dared voice it. There was probably a Stasi file on me as it was. "Comrade Heidi Baumann is daily engaged in suspicious counterrevolutionary staring contest with the Anti-Fascist Protection Rampart," it probably said.

As I grew up in the shadow of the Wall, under the flag of the hammer and compass, I continued to visit that section of the Wall every day that I could. Some of the details changed over the years. The Young Pioneer uniform I often wore during my visits to the Wall gave way to an FDJ uniform. My method of traveling there changed as well, from a child's skip to a clunky Trabant. On the rare days that I couldn't manage a visit to the Wall, I felt a sharp stab of guilt, as though I had abandoned someone calling for help. But what sense did that make? I wasn't making a difference just by standing there.

So it went until the twenty-eighth year of my life. Following reforms in the Soviet Union, Poland, and Hungary, our own hardline government finally began to bend to the people's will. Erich Honecker, our intransigent fossil of a leader, was ousted. And then, on the evening of November 9, 1989, Günter Schabowski announced on television that the border with the West was now open. After all this time, could it really be true?

I went to see if it was. It wasn't exactly an original thought. Huge crowds were gathering at the checkpoints in the Wall to see if the border was really opening. The border guards seemed to know nothing about any change in policy, but they eventually gave in and let the people pass through. They were greeted warmly by the people on the other side, the people whom our government would have us believe were "fascists." Soon, people were climbing over the Wall, but no one was shooting at them. The Wall had become harmless.

I ran to the section of the Wall to which I had always been drawn. A hand reached down to help me up and I took it. As I came up onto the Wall, I gazed into the face of a twenty-eight-year-old woman. She was... me. A different me. A Western me, with a mass of curly hair atop her head and a most peculiar outfit composed of bright, neon colors. We embraced as we came together on top of the Wall.

As I would soon learn, she was Marlene Baumann, the identical twin sister I had never known. She had been with relatives in the West on that day in 1961 when the Wall was built. No doubt hoping to spare us the pain of separation, our respective guardians had both chosen to never tell us about the other.

And yet, we had somehow been able to sense the other. For as long as we could remember, we had felt the same pull. On every day that we could, we had stood directly across from each other, as close as we could be with the Wall in the way.

2017 marks twenty-eight years since the fall of the Berlin Wall, the same number of years for which the Wall stood.

LOCAL HEADLINE by Lauri Leonetti

Thursday, April 20, 2017, Beaverton, OR –

I wasn't there. I don't know her. I have no clue of her hair color, body shape or clothing style. In the initial news report I heard, she was listed as an unidentified, twenty-six-year-old woman, and although I didn't suspect she might be someone I know, I felt a connection with her. Why?

Likely, I've so often passed the intersection where she was hit by the freight train, I can visualize myself at the juncture, observing the horrific event. Possibly, my memory of actually having witnessed a similar accident contributes to the yoke which now ties me to her.

As a young twenty-something, traveling home on a Portland city bus, I'd been idly gazing out the left-side window against which I leaned after a tiring day of work. The bus had stopped to discharge and reload passengers, but the traffic beside me continued to pulse in the flow of lives needing to persevere. The thin, dark-haired teenager leapt off the bus steps, rounding its nose in a sprint to cross the busy street. I caught the movement with a subconscious side glance, realizing in hindsight I'd sensed a premonition of the coming incident. With his speed, I presumed he lacked the leisure to look at anything but his intended destination, with no thought to—or maybe no parental instruction in—performing the *'left, right, left'* traffic check, drilled into my street-crossing routine from childhood. My view blocked, I did not see his body cross in front of the bus, but peripherally to my left, I did see the school bus approach alongside us, and the impact as he emerged onto the roadway.

Despite the pre-alarm hints, it all happened so quickly that the shock gut-punched me into full-sensory mode. In my following night- and day-mares, the *'thunk'* sound haunted me the most. The scattering of books, pens and papers from the backpack he carried spawned my sharpest recurring image, with focus on a notebook which remained splayed in the street as we passed the site, after the paramedics arrived and the police allowed my bus to continue on its route.

According to today's accounts, comparable to the boy's tragedy, the female pedestrian perpetrated her collision with the train, probably unwittingly, but nonetheless self-induced. The railroad-crossing arms, flashing lights, bells, and walk signals all functioned properly. Witnesses attested to hearing the engineer blow the train's horn as the conductor yelled from the engine walkway to warn her as well. Many claimed they noticed her looking down at her phone as she proceeded along the crosswalk into the locomotive's path.

My reaction to hearing this explanation paralleled the horror of my bus memories. Although I don't tend to engross myself in the use of my phone, especially not at the risk of being unsafely distracted in a public situation, I *have* shown poor judgment or behaved unthinkingly in detrimental ways. I believe very few people could say they haven't.

I've chosen to eat that extra brownie, skip a workout, or not go the doctor when I suspect an ache to be abnormal. These behaviors can lead to a negative outcome, along with staying up too late to finish watching a movie, or getting caught up in scrolling through Facebook posts when I'm later sorry I didn't spend my precious time more productively, like honing my writing skills. These poor choices affect me personally, but even though I use Bluetooth when I speak on the phone while driving, I've allowed myself to be preoccupied with opening a snack bar package, with changing a CD, or with sidetracking my attention for an extra scan of a crash memorial I see along the road. As humans, we often make decisions—or mistakes—which affect others, sometimes disastrously, perhaps much more profoundly than we'd imagine, and frequently when we're not even aware.

This young woman's actions caused herself (and her family and friends) the most anguish, but I, too, feel sorrow when I contemplate her misfortune and imagine them gathered in a hospital room, wondering if she'd ever walk again. Besides vicariously aching with empathy for her, it triggers uncomfortable emotions from my past, fears for my future, and distress for ways in which humanity is degenerating with advancing technology, busier lifestyles, and less regard for others.

Especially in our current state of political, societal and global hyperawareness, with so many news sources reporting stories which terrorize, anger, and cause despondency, my sense of association with this woman illustrates an analogous bond I'm feeling with much of what's happening in our country and the world. What are we doing, or allowing to transpire, as we blindly scurry through the busyness of our days, rush around trying to accomplish *'important things'*, and become reliant on technology and the distractions it provides? As we dash to appointments, ignoring the downcast faces around us, or hasten to use social media to criticize someone who appears dissimilar from us or from our social circles or ideologies, we head into the pathway of a destructive sociopolitical train.

When noting that regulated safety systems, and efforts by Portland & Western Railroad personnel, didn't prevent her perilous stroll into danger's way, I wondered if any bystanders had considered running after this soon-to-be victim, to ensure her awareness, to restrain or pull her back. I mused whether I would have had the wherewithal to have attempted a rescue. Numerous articles and video clips covering the incident mentioned witnesses observing her looking at her phone, but I heard no reference to anyone physically trying to stop her. I hope if that's true, they simply did not have time, rather than their being too distracted or self-absorbed themselves.

Listen photographed by Carolyn Adams

SECRET LIVES by Robin Layne

"Friends may not say they love each other, but they very often do." Lily paused at the typewriter, recalling her best friend Charity saying, "I love you just the way you are." Lily had been so thrilled to hear she was loved, she'd run through an open field across the street, thinking that if anyone asked her if she had ever been in love, she would answer yes.

Lily says best friends are people who tell each other everything. When she and Charity aren't talking at school, walking each other home, or sleeping over, they talk on the phone until a parent orders, "Hang up! Somebody may be trying to call." The two have been best friends since junior high. They're both writers, and they both like to let their characters out in the real world. They do this by thinking through the characters' points of view, talking to one another in their unique voices, and so on.

Outsiders don't know. Once a fellow high schooler said at lunch break, "What's with this? Every time you two meet, you hand each other notes." The two conspirators just smiled at each other and said nothing. If the third girl had snatched the notes out of their hands, she would have found two long letters written in different handwriting, signed with names that might have been neither Lily's nor Charity's. Further reading would have made little sense to the intruder, for these letters are written by people who live in another dimension—whose lives sometimes intertwine with the girls themselves.

I ought to know. I'm one of those characters.

My name is Matthew. Lily wanted to call someone that. I won't give you my last name because it's embarrassing. She got it from a phone book, but it looked unpronounceable until Charity suggested she add a vowel; they thought the name was interesting, and a little naughty, like me.

This is why I'm here: Some time back, during a discussion with Charity, Lily decided to pattern a new character after a drug dealer she'd killed off in a story; she wanted the new one to become a Christian. She relates to her characters in real time, an approach she got from Charity, who's always the leader. One fateful day, the drug dealer's greenish eyes stared back at Lily from a mustached face on a Winston ad. She was drawn in by the whole photo. That's where I began. Just how I'd mend my wicked ways, Lily imagined she'd work out over time. First, she got to know me through conversations in her head, which she wrote down. Then she let me loose at the typewriter to begin an autobiography. Of course, at times she "let me out" to talk to Charity or one of Charity's "people," as she calls them.

The character Charity spends the most time on is Hotch, the Scottish drummer of a rock'n'roll band. He speaks in a higher voice than Charity, with a strong brogue, so it's easy to tell when he's out. One day in the high school art room, Hotch'd demanded to know why Lily wouldn't have a romance with one of her own "people" like the one Charity has with him. Those two were well underway with a child and a marriage in the other dimension.

Lily felt cornered (I know because I occupy the same brain). She finally admitted that it would mean "doing *that*" (she meant sex but wouldn't say the word), even if it was only in her mind. She wanted to wait for marriage in the outside world.

But something happened after she met womanizing, drug-abusing me. Lily decided *she* would be the one to lead me to Christ. And to do that, she would have to do something she had never done before: come into *my* world—have an identity in the other dimension. I mocked her attempts to reform me, kissed her forehead like a Judas, and took off to get drunk. Lily lay in her bed listening to love songs on the radio and thinking of me. I got into a fight in the bar with a guy who smashed my forehead into the wall. Another man took me home and put me in his spare room. I woke up feeling like a truck had run me over, and saw Lily sitting next to the bed watching over me. When I gathered she'd been in that chair all night, I said, "You're one hell of a woman." The fifteen-year-old had always wanted to hear that.

Rosebud drawn by Robin Layne

Impressed by her love, I did convert after a while, and I quit smoking while occupying myself with her kisses. Lily's family said she was too old to have an imaginary friend, so she stopped talking about me to them. We got married the day after she turned sixteen. In my dimension, we settled into a little house in Spokane, Washington, where I set up a photography studio, and we decided to have a little girl. Since my wife is also my creator, we can control things like that.

The more time Lily's spent looking through my eyes, letting me lounge around her home, and listening to music that fits me, the more real I've become. Her theory is that I occupy a different part of her brain than the rest of her personality.

Since both now have imaginary husbands, the two girls have grown closer than ever. I talked with Charity in the high school darkroom the other day. As the print developed under the dim orange light, the tall blond girl sure looked good...

I guess some people are slow to change. Even imaginary lovers.

SHE USED TO TALK TOO MUCH by Sheila Deeth

She used to talk too much. He always said so, right from the start. But he smiled so she imagined it no more important than getting freckles in summer. After all, he talked a lot too while they endlessly set the world to rights—history, politics, civil liberties, all the way up to religion—nothing taboo, not even death and taxes. They argued of course, when they disagreed. But they'd met at university; they were both intelligent, and they knew to always respect each other's point of view.

They still talked as a couple when they were married. Cooking together in the tiny kitchen of their first apartment, they squeezed past each other to reach the fridge and stove while discussing family hang-ups and what the future might hold. Then they had kids. She stayed home to cook and clean and care for them while he went out to work. The whole world changed.

She still talked then, in the chatter of two-year-olds from morning to dusk and again when they cried in the night. It was bliss meeting for coffee and talking with other moms sometimes, even if all they discussed were toilet training, schools and what to do if the baby were choking. When her husband came home, she kept the kids out of his way, whispering they should keep their voices down. Daddy was tired. Daddy wanted instant obedience while his children wanted attention. So she tried to keep the peace, made dinner, washed and tidied up. "Can it wait? In a minute. When I've got the kids to bed." She wished she had more interesting things to say, but by now he was deep in the paper or the news, or he was going out.

They didn't talk to each other much, but she still talked too much. He told her so. When the children were noisy it was because they copied her. When they sulked and were quiet, she should have brought them up better—better able to communicate. When they were silent, she shouldn't spoil his peace with wasteful words.

The kids grew into teenagers with college entrance and tests. Their father lectured them and they learned, each in turn, to sit to attention. He dictated how they should write and how much they should write. He filled their silence with words. She interfered, of course, still trying to help, still hoping to keep a peace which the children learned to attain without any words.

Sometimes he spoke to her. He told her his office was busy and he needed his home life calm. He taught her not to take him for granted, so she cut grass, did yardwork, built bookshelves, and fixed dripping taps. He even asked her advice on occasion, then she knew she had to guess what answer was required: Don't disagree. Don't contradict. Don't say he's wrong when he's asking you to say yes. But she couldn't read his mind.

When she asked his help, he didn't hear. He couldn't read her mind and tell when he was supposed to listen. Then she felt old. A neighbor asked if the man was her oldest son.

Perhaps it was having children that aged her. Perhaps it was the years at home, helping them learn, guiding their faltering steps, sharing their concerns and holding their hands. Or perhaps she really was useless, even if the kids still asked her advice. If they thanked her she called it coincidence. If her husband thanked her, she grabbed the treat like a baby clutching unexpected sweetness to its lips.

One day she sat with the dog, playing back recordings on TV. She had a whole collection from when they were young. Her twenties voice spoke clearly describing the scene. "Those red doors are the hanger at the airport. It's our little boy's birthday today." As she listened and watched, as the years went by, she noticed that voice became silent. Views were accompanied only by whispering sounds of traffic and wind. Unspeaking children sat on the sofa; she didn't call their names. She didn't even call the dog, just zoomed the camera in as he played then stood motionless, equally silent in the snow.

The youngest boy came home after school. She gave him a drink and settled him to his homework then walked the dog, nodding silently at people on the street. When her husband came home she made dinner for herself and her son. Just a sandwich for Dad because he'd eaten at work. She couldn't even ask if her cooking was okay.

They watched TV and she didn't talk, because talking would distract him and she knew she talked too much.

SIBLINGS by Jean Harkin

I ask them to not cause
Each other grief, but pause
To think before they speak
In anger or in pique.

He to stop and listen,
She to quiet her chatter,
He not to fuss and mix in
When she begins her patter
(It really doesn't matter!)

It's not that I want quiet
But rather, I'd like peace.
How to stop the riot
And make the quarrels cease?

Siblings photographed by Jean Harkin

SOME ASSEMBLY REQUIRED by Richard David Bach

Late One Christmas Eve

"Ouch, dammit, I can't get this out." Chester sucked on his torn thumb.

Valerie leaned over and took the plastic piece from him. "Here… let me try," she said. "Why are you taking this section apart? You just put it together."

"Because I was supposed to put this stupid door-jamb in first. I should have sent this thing back as soon as I saw *'some assembly required'* printed on the box. Look at these instructions. Can you read them? They were probably written in Hindi and translated by a Croatian. Oh, dammit, now I'm getting blood all over them." Chester sighed. "I wish Grampa were here… he'd know how to put this thing together. Besides… he'd have a Band-Aid in his wallet."

Chester Morgan sat cross-legged on the living room carpet, sucking his wounded thumb, surrounded by more than half of the original 482 pieces of the doll house that would be the highlight of Kellie's Christmas, even if this year her Grampa wouldn't be there when she came running downstairs on Christmas morning. He picked up a piece of the doll house's living room wall, turning it over and over trying to figure out where it went, without being distracted by the wallpaper patterns.

"Hey, Val, look how the surface of this piece reflects these weird colors from your silly tree." Across the room the tree—a cunningly crafted seven-foot faux noble fir with a prominent *'made in China'* label—glowed with a purple aura and bathed everything in mauve tones. Kellie and Valerie had opted for pink and lavender. There were only two colors on Kellie's three-year old palette—and their trip to the mall had produced $85 worth of pink plastic ornaments, lavender tree lights, and pink and lavender plaid ribbon. Chester had pantomimed *'gag me with a spoon'* when he first walked in and saw the display, while Kellie bounced up and down in self-satisfied glee.

"I miss him too, Honey." Valerie knelt behind Chester and wrapped her arms around his chest. "Christmas just won't be the same this year without Grampa. Can I get you a bandage for that?"

He pulled his thumb out of his mouth just long enough to look at the cut. "Yeah, I guess I should put something on it… it won't quit bleeding." It was beginning to throb and he couldn't concentrate on the instructions. "I can't believe he's not here. He's always been here and it never occurred to me that he wouldn't always be."

He looked up. "Hey Val, that's Grampa's favorite." Valerie's mix of holiday songs had been shuffling all evening, and now Eartha Kitt's *'Santa Baby'* came smoldering out of the I-Pod sitting on top of the unemployed piano in the far corner. "Grampa always said that Eartha Kitt could get him off his death bed with that song. It was one of the reasons Christmas was his favorite time of the year and why he brought such cheer to the holidays." Chester shrugged and rummaged around in the pieces on the carpet. "Have you seen the tiny little curtain rod that goes over the living room window?"

"Here it is." Valerie leaned over, handed him the piece, and kissed him on the cheek. "You know what I can't understand... with his contempt for religion, how come the big deal over Christmas?"

"Oh, that's easy. It's the winter solstice. He'd've sacrificed a goat to Odin if the Humane Society wouldn't object, and if people want to brighten up the season with a 2000-year-old fairytale as an excuse to go shopping, that'd be okay with him too. He loved the decorations, the music, the excitement in the air... but you know what turned him on the most...? Shopping for Christmas presents for all his grandchildren." Chester paused and glanced toward the top of the stairs. "And now, a great-granddaughter."

Chester sighed and looked at all the lovingly wrapped packages under the pink tree. "You know, Val, he never admitted it, but I think he was just a little disappointed when we all grew up and really wanted money or gift certificates instead of those dopey toys he used to order online. His favorite website opened with *'Welcome back, Grampa Richard, what can we put in your basket today?'* and he especially loved the 'educational' toys..." Chester held up his fingers in the quotation mark sign "... that would turn us all into little geniuses."

Valerie stretched, swiveling at the hips with her back arched and her hands up in the air. "Yeah, I wish I had known him back then. He bought this doll house for Kellie last summer, knowing full well that he wouldn't be here to put it together; and he was so excited when he called to tell me that he had found it on the internet and that FedEx would have it here in about a week.... oops, look out!"

Doll house pieces scattered in all directions as Kellie's new calico pounced on the round pink plastic ball she had stripped from a bottom branch and had dribbled across the living room rug. Valerie laughed, scooped up the kitten with one hand and picked up the surprisingly intact ornament with the other. "Hey, these plastic ornaments are great. Gramma's glass ones would have been in a million pieces with this cat on the loose."

Chester used a forefinger to nudge the doll-sized queen bed in the master bedroom to the right a quarter inch to make room for a bedside table, knocking over a miniature lamp in the process. "Damn… I'm such a fumble-fingers." He turned to Valerie. "Do you think Kellie will be okay with Grampa not here when she gets up in the morning?"

"Oh, I hope so," sighed Valerie, spreading a postage stamp-sized hooked rug on the den floor. "She's pretty solid, but she's so darned deep. Sometimes I don't have the faintest idea what's going on in that little mind of hers. I guess we'll just have to…"

The phone rang. They looked at each other and Chester looked at the clock over Valerie's shoulder. *1:34 AM.* He jumped up on the second ring, realized that the phone was nowhere in sight by the third ring, and found it on the couch under a pile of red and green wrapping paper by the fourth.

"Hello."

"Hi, Kiddo, how's it going?"

"Grampa… where are you?"

"We just cleared customs at Orly, and I'm waiting for a cab to take us downtown. I can't wait to see the Eiffel Tower all lit up for Christmas."

"How was your flight?"

"Great… uneventful… the best kind. Gramma wanted to turn around and come right back home because she misses you all so much, but I'm going to love every minute of Christmas in Paris. It sure will be different. Did you get the doll house put together okay without me?"

Chester didn't quite know how best to respond, but before he could come up with an answer, Grampa Richard changed the subject. "Oh, oh…here comes a cab. Give Valerie and Kellie big hugs for us, and do me a favor…? Call everyone and let them know we got here safely?"

"Okay, Grampa, we'll do that. You and Gramma have a wonderful time, and Kellie's gonna love the doll house. We love you and we miss you, and oh… happy winter solstice."

Chester punched the off button on the telephone, leaned over to Valerie and kissed her lightly on the lips. "Well, I guess we're on our own. Now, where did I put that little coffee table I had a moment ago?"

A SONG OF ETERNAL FLAME by Susan Apurado

The mouth of San Francisco Bay
Speaks of its magnificent beauty,
That could've swept our hearts away.

Seated there on a rocky surface,
Sniffed the salty sweat of the ocean,
Taciturnly traced the pockets
In our memory bank.

Relentless winds,
Glued beneath our sultry skin.
Nothin' could stop, two hearts in flame!

Had it been a bitter gall of ten years?
Across in that island, called Alcatraz.
You used to write me a letter
About your life, passion, and all the jazz

Ah, a Nightmare! We made it over.
Woke up with you, my Beau,
And slipped the ring on my finger.

A euphoric mile calculated our fate.
Two lovers once, torn apart into darkness
Yet the distance spanned by the golden gate
Where dreams came true; sealed with bliss.

Treacherous tides…
Flushed our bitter memories, left to die.
Sung a song of our love; eternally resides.

Painted by Susan Apurado

WONDER

Wonderful Friendship photographed by Judy Beaston

EARTH WONDER by Jean Harkin

I wonder at spring and the birds every year
As they flock to the limbs of my dogwood tree,
Enhancing the branches as if it were Christmas—
Alighting and flighting, their colors vivacious.

I wonder at trees and the blossoms that spring
From the buds that uncurl, unfurling new beauty,
The fresh breath of green and touch of yellow
In bushes and branches of the weeping willow.

I wonder at beauty, so varied and fragile—
Life's chain that connects bug, fish, bird and mammal,
Stone, leaves and water under blue heaven.

People, come share the wonder of living
This moment of NOW on earth that we're given.

Photograph by Karen Alexander-Brown

THOUGHTS OF WONDER by Susan Apurado

If there is a rainbow after the rain
Why can't it last long to wipe out the pain?

If in springtime the flowers blossom
Why can't they stay long past on winter storm?

If the greens forage in the summer sway
Why would the October sun kiss them away?

If smiles and laughter bring gladness
Why would the river of tears flood in stillness?

If life is precious in spiritual theory
Why is someone's breath taken away?

If mortals we are, to the dust we go
Why in life's pain do we need to go through?

Photograph by Susan Apurado

WONDER by Jessie Collins

Wonder is such an interesting word. It can be used quite casually as a verb, as in "I wonder what to do about this." But *wonder* as a noun can mean something very profound. This variety of wonder is what I am thinking about now. There have been countless examples of it in my long life, but I shall write about just a few special ones.

I look back to when I was just eleven years old. Something very special was to happen at our church, and all my friends were talking about the lovely new dresses they were going to wear. I kept out of these conversations because I knew my parents couldn't afford to buy me a new dress. We had just heard that I had passed the examination to go to grammar school, and there was all my school uniform to buy. Then one day my mother came home with a bag over her arm. "Look what's in here," she said to me. It was a lovely pink silk party dress. The wonder of it just overwhelmed me. My lovely parents had given me something that I would not have dared to ask for.

I'm moving on to the time when I was eighteen and had recently left school. University was just around the corner, and that might have been sufficient cause for wonder, but something unexpected and very special was about to turn my world upside down. I had become friendly with a young man who had returned home from the Far East after years as a prisoner of war. I knew I was getting far too fond of him, but it wasn't going to lead to anything, because he was eight years older than me and was just being nice to a schoolgirl. Out of the blue one day he told me how he felt about me, and oh! the wonder of it all! Life took on a new dimension. A love affair that lasted more than half a century had begun.

Obviously there were many moments of wonder during the years that followed. Some stand out from the others. I remember standing with my father at the church door and looking toward where that wonderful man waited for me at the altar on our wedding day. Because it was a mixed marriage (I, a Methodist, marrying my Roman Catholic fiancé in his church) no music was allowed. I had felt sorry about this, but when that wonderful moment arrived I just felt that all the bells of heaven were ringing as I walked up the aisle toward him. Definitely a moment of wonder.

Three times during our married life I felt the wonder of the first stirrings of a mother's love as I held my new baby in my arms. Those dear children have brought me many moments of wonder as the years have passed by, as children, and in their adult lives. Two weddings and one ordination to the priesthood were extra special, and of course the lovely moments of holding my grandchildren for the first time.

At last there came the time when I thought there would be no more wonder in my life, the day my dear husband died. Nearly eighteen years have gone by since then, and I have discovered that life can still hold moments of wonder. One of the highlights of my life was the wonderful day three years ago when my son who is a priest received me into the Roman Catholic Church. I think perhaps the greatest element of wonder that day was the amazing feeling that after eighty-five years as a Methodist I had come home at last.

I have seen so much wonder on the faces of children and it has always thrilled me to see it. Not only my own children and grandchildren but many boys and girls whom I have taught have given me those special moments. However, I cannot finish writing this essay without mentioning the greatest wonder of all, a wonder that is new every morning—the wonder that our Lord, whose family encompasses countless millions, cares enough about me to be close to me every day, never more than a prayer away. Glory to His Name!

Glenwood photographed by Carolyn Adams

117

WISE FELINE by Judy Beaston

Calico cat pads on silent paws
through neighborhood gardens,
across sun-steamed streets
her destination a wooded meadow
where cool shade provides rest,
while thick foliage allows stealth
during dinnertime hunts.

Calico on the Walk photographed by Judy Beaston

MAP IN THE AIR by Carolyn Adams

Gulls and terns cut the wind
with razor wings,
heading south from shore.

I follow
their compass,
their map in the air.

Ten miles out.
Twenty.

We row the sky,
past the shoal
where minnows school,
over that sandbar
where cockles are thick.

I hit the water,
take a fish in my mouth.
I eat,
and feel the fish go still.

Its rich salt and flesh
become
my wings, my beak,
my quickened eye.

Jade Waters painted by Karen Alexander-Brown

119

LEFT BEHIND by Sheila Deeth

Do you remember, little girl,
The first time you saw them hold hands and they weren't holding you
Because you
Were watching behind the window glass while they
Walked up the drive?

They opened the door, came inside, still holding hands;
You fitted yourself in between where it seemed
You'd be safe at last and free
And you didn't cry.

Do you remember, nearly teen,
When they stopped needing your hands in theirs?
You ran and stared
Through window glass—such scenes to wonder at;
Blue flowing seas; and you were free
To see—do you remember they
Weren't holding hands that day,
And you felt cold inside?

They held hands at your wedding though.
You wondered why; which one feared which
Would run away and fly;
Or was it you?

Do you remember, blushing bride,
Holding his
Hand? You stood inside looking out
Through the window glass of your honeymoon suite, you
Wondering why he
Didn't want to fasten his hand on yours
Except when he couldn't be seen.

Do you remember
Holding your children's hands,
Wondering which of you, you feared,
Would run away and fly?

And now, remember all those hands
While yours hang empty—all the world holds hands
Except for you.
Look through the window glass again and watch
As blushing pink turns back to blue; you
Didn't run away at all. It's you
They left behind.

Heaven's In Here photographed by Carolyn Adams

IN AWE OF NATURE'S SPLENDOR by Judy Beaston

Waterfall's ceaseless spill
over cliff's rocky edge
creates a steamy mist
against today's azure sky,

water flows like sheets of blue silk
woven with silver threads,
lines that dance, at times,
fall straight at others

before one final plunge
into the deep pool below,
a bouquet of rebounded drops
cascading across nearby rocks.

Whirlpools twirl leaves,
twigs, bits of whipped spray,
a frantic battle, it seems,
between demise and release

before currents carry remnants
away from the turmoil,
onward to calmer streams,
their long trek back home.

Grow, collage by Carolyn Adams

POINT OF VIEW

Bedroom photographed by Carolyn Adams

HALO IN THE DARK by Karen Alexander-Brown

"I have others, you know."

"Others? Oh! You mean…" Brad's fingers gingerly circled his own nose around the same general location as the nose ring on Jolene's face.

"Yes. In case you were wondering."

Brad blushed in spite of himself. He thought he had been discrete. Watching her slender hands work deftly to compact and fold the massive mixture of multi-colored ingredients into one large flour tortilla, he contemplated where she might have other rings on her body. She wrapped the burrito in a paper-lined foil wrapper and closed it with a sticker. When she handed it to him, it felt warm and heavy like a newborn baby's body… or a woman's ample breast.

"What color?" Jolene's hands shielded her eyes from him.

"Uh, chestnut?"

"Blue. Deep blue. I didn't think you'd noticed."

His embarrassed grin was his confession.

"Do I pay you or up front?" he asked.

"Up front. They're anxious to close the registers so you'd better hurry."

"Thanks."

He hesitated as Jolene swept the stray bits to the floor and lifted a bin of spicy shredded meat out of the counter to begin the process of closing down for the night. Brad sauntered toward the registers. As he was paying for his burrito he joked with the checkout crew. When he glanced back toward the Burrito Bar, Jolene was gone.

The wet parking lot sparkled under the street lamps after a day of misty rains. Brad pulled up his hood and hunched his shoulders against the moisture. His car lights blinked at him when he unlocked the doors with the remote. He slid into the driver's seat and pulled the heavy door shut.

The fragrance of the burrito was too much to resist. He tore open the foil cover and sank his teeth into rich Mexican spices offset by crunchy lettuce and a flour tortilla. As the windows steamed up from the moisture emanating from Brad and the burrito, he devoured the heavy meal in silence in the dark cocoon of his car. The rain began to fall harder against the windshield.

The back seat and trunk were filled with what he could salvage after the eviction—a 32 inch flat screen television, his MacBook Pro computer, a suitcase and a duffel bag of clothes, his books for classes, his notes, some kitchen utensils and pots, a backpack and an alarm clock. Unpaid bills sent to his defunct address littered the passenger floor. Try as he might, he could not find a place to rent that would fit his budget, despite working two jobs. His friends were already living with multiple people to an apartment. Brad looked around the car and wondered if he could survive winter living in it.

Three sharp raps on the passenger window made him jump. The door opened and Jolene slipped into the passenger seat, dripping with rain. She looked at Brad and offered her ring-filled hand to him.

"Jolene."

"Brad." He shook her soft, warm hand as her eyes took in the state of his car.

"Newly evicted? Or do you live in here?"

"Newly evicted."

"Bummer. Got anywhere to go?"

"Nope, not a clue."

A few moments passed as she sized him up. He guessed that she was a few years older than he.

"Tell you what. I just missed my bus and I don't want to stand in the dark in the rain waiting for the next one. I'll buy you a beer if you'll give me a ride. The bar up the street stays open late. That is, if you don't have anywhere else to be."

"At your service, Jolene." The thought of a reprieve from his desperate situation sounded good. Jolene's company sounded good.

Brad started the engine and put on the defroster to clear the fogged up windows. The interior of his car smelled of burrito and wet clothes. The car turned a circle in the parking lot with the crunch of wet tires and they headed up the street.

The bar was brightly lit and had a few customers seated there. The bartender greeted Jolene with familiarity.

"Hey Joe. Give us two of your IPA's, okay?" She turned to Brad. "That okay with you?"

"Sure, thanks!"

"I just might have a possible solution to your housing situation. One of my housemates just left out of the blue and we need someone to cover his rent. Tell me something about yourself…"

To Brad, the backlit glow of the bar formed a halo around Jolene. He wondered if he'd ever have a chance to discover the location of her other rings, but for now she was his guardian angel.

Photograph by Karen Alexander-Brown

POINTS OF VIEW ON A CAFÉ MEETING by Jean Harkin

That woman's been watching me. She reminds me of someone—not sure who. Somebody I've seen somewhere—not sure where. I've not been here before, so it's from somewhere else. Maybe she just reminds me of someone. Oh, she's leaving—uh, oh, coming this way. Maybe she recognizes me too. Hopefully not from too long ago. Of course, I'm bad with names anyway. Does she know mine? I hope not. Here she is, better stand up and greet her. Oh—she stumbles. Something on the floor? Or something wrong with her? She's blushing, so I smile to reassure her. She's pretty. We both sit down. She smiles back. Pretty smile, even teeth. She says...

* * *

The café is not crowded. A few groups sit together at tables. Two people sit alone at their separate tables—a man at one, woman at another. The dark-haired, stoutly built man, slouching in a blue windbreaker jacket, taps an index finger on the oak laminate tabletop and stirs his coffee with a spoon in the other hand. He keeps glancing at the woman, then down at the coffee, as if he is thinking or remembering.

The thin woman, with yellow-blond frizzy hair restrained under a purple beanie, is watching the man, although she keeps checking her phone. She clicks and appears to be texting, then waits, looking up at the man then darting her eyes back to the phone. She taps a finale on the phone, then puts it into her purse. She turns to grab her jacket that was draped over the chair, gets up, and heads over to the man's table. As she reaches for the chair, her foot slips on a slick spot on the floor. She recovers quickly, smiles, and sits down.

* * *

..."Hi Tim. Do you remember me from high school?"

"You look familiar, but I don't recall your name. I'm habitually bad with names. And I'm not Tim, by the way."

Hand to her mouth. "Oh—you look like Tim Sudor—from Palmridge High School." She pauses. "Ages ago." She allows a faint smile.

"Sudor? That's my last name—but not Tim."

A puzzled expression, then, "Really?" Staring at him, she says, "This is strange."

He sips his coffee. "Strange, yeah."

"I mean really strange—you look so much. . ."

He interrupts with a dismissive chuckle, "Maybe it was my cousin—or something, back then."

* * *

She hasn't mentioned that she's just checked *Tim Sudor* on her phone and found an interesting link. Her unblinking stare persists, as if she is trying to look into the past through his eyes. He looks away through the wide windowpane to the parking lot where his car waits for him to escape.

"Did you have a cousin named Tim at Palmridge about sixteen years ago?" she asks in a soft voice.

"N-no, that is I don't know where he went to high school. I didn't know him, just heard he was my cousin." The man wonders why she persists. "Let's just say I must look like my cousin Tim, and that's that."

"Okay," she says, a tiny frown appearing between her eyebrows. She would like to ask further, but thinks better of it, at least for the moment.

The man, his face pale as though he avoids sunshine, thinks the polite move would be to offer to buy her coffee or tea, but he'd rather not prolong this meeting. He is feeling beads of sweat under his shirt collar. He looks at his wristwatch and says, "Well, I'm afraid I need to be going. I have a meeting."

She notices he looks uncomfortable and wonders if he's just making an excuse to get away. She thinks he must really know about his cousin Tim and would not like to continue this conversation. Maybe it's true what she found out about Tim Sudor—that he was convicted of auto theft and kidnapping soon after high school and served prison time.

***

The man sips a draw of coffee, then sets down the mug as he rises from his chair. Hand shaking, he grabs the spoon and crumpled napkin with a jerk that makes the spoon clatter to the table and the wad of paper fall into the mug. "Goddamit," he mutters, then sucks in his breath, gathering the tableware. The blond woman's lips curl into a little smile; her bird-like attentive eyes search the man's face to see what he'll do next.

He thinks, *This busybody is trouble,* and says, "I'm really sorry I have to leave so quickly before we could get acquainted." His attempted smile comes out a grimace.

"I'm sorry too," she responds and thinks, *This was just getting interesting.* The man turns away, and she watches him head toward the exit. She muses, *He never asked my name and didn't tell me his first name. Very interesting indeed!*

Tim doesn't look back. As he nears the door, he drops the mug, spoon, and napkin into the trash bin. *Last time I'm coming here,* he thinks. *That bitch almost got me!*

Java Time photographed at Java Lounge by Judy Beaston

UNTITLED by Susan Apurado

Summer breezes
Have long been gone
The fountain of youth
Is melancholy done

Sunny days thought were forever
When time slips away
It won't hold us back together
Put the foot forward and head on

In life, regret is merely a futile
Just do best of what you can bring
When the knife of darkness steals
Think it is only a temporary thing

We chose this path to walk this far
Keep your eyes on the road and feel the sign
Somewhere all along, you'll see a star
To guide your life and make you shine…

Summer Breezes photographed by Susan Apurado

DREAMS COME TRUE WITH HOPE AND FAITH
by Joe Mendez

The inspiring true story of a man with a dream who moved to New York City to discover himself.

There are some unforgettable dreams so strange or so beautiful you find them difficult to share with others. But one dream I must tell about, for I believe it was from God.

Some years ago when I was living in Portland, Oregon, I dreamed I was a famous musician. A young reporter from New York came to interview me. She was beautiful, with lustrous auburn hair and warm, friendly eyes with crinkly laugh lines.

I awoke with my heart pounding. Though I doubted I would ever be famous, I felt certain that God had shown me the woman I would marry. I called her my Dream Princess.

Marriage, however, seemed distant. Even though I was 39, I still hadn't made much of my life. My ambition was to become a published writer. I had written stories, plays, poems and books, but none had seen print. To support myself, I worked for an auto dealership, washing and selling cars. In my spare time I refereed at school athletic events.

Because I firmly believed the promise that God would guide me, I decided to move to New York City. That's where the publishers are. Friends and most of my nine brothers and sisters ridiculed me. "You need contacts, Joe," warned one. "The city will eat you up," said another, laughing. "You'll be glad to come back to Portland."

My answer was to buy a one-way Amtrak ticket to New York. In late June 1991, I boarded the train after saying goodbye to my sister, brother-in-law and nephew. One of my two suitcases held all the books, stories, plays and poems I had written, along with $400.

On July 4, I arrived in bustling Penn Station. I set down my suitcases to check the hotel address. When I leaned over to pick them up, the one with my manuscripts and money was gone! Astonished and dumbfounded, I found a policeman. All he could recommend was to file a report. "Welcome to New York," someone said, snickering. All I had left was $100 in my wallet. I checked into a hotel and started looking for work. A few days later, on an evening stroll, I was mugged. I lost my cash and ID. I couldn't believe it.

Twice in one week! "You gotta be careful," advised the hotel clerk, shrugging his shoulders.

Meanwhile, no publisher was hiring. I searched for any kind of job, but it seemed hopeless. I felt I was at least becoming streetwise, until I went to the restroom in Grand Central Station. Once again I was mugged. This time I was slammed against the wall, and a shiny blade was pressed against my stomach before my assailant fled. Penniless, I went to Traveler's Aid. They advised me to call my family. *No way*, I vowed. I couldn't face the "I told you so's." With no place to live, I joined New York's homeless and hungry. The aroma wafting from restaurants tied my stomach in knots. I stared hungrily at half-eaten food in street-corner trash baskets.

Someone said that the Church of St. Agnes near Grand Central Station had a drop-in center where some 400 people gathered to eat every night. I felt fortunate to join them, but I didn't feel right sleeping there. It was still summer, so I slept in doorways and on park benches. Sometimes I rode the subway or walked the streets all night. I soon learned to wrap myself in newspapers and lie on top of cardboard to stave off the night chill. But finding a job without a home address or identification was hopeless. That was the worst of it—feeling useless, not having anywhere to be, getting awakened by footsteps of lucky people hurrying to work.

Sometimes I thought of my Dream Princess, but now she too seemed a fading illusion. Desolate days blended into a gray emptiness. Some evenings found me in an all-night McDonald's near Times Square, writing my thoughts in a notebook. Occasionally the manager let me sleep in the closed-off upstairs section.

Fall was coming on and one cold night I trudged through Herald Square. Despite the crowd, I felt alone. Sick at heart, I looked up into the murky sky and wondered if God had forgotten me. I thought of the Psalms my mom had had me memorize, in which the psalmist continually expressed his faith even in the grimmest circumstances. Leaning against an iron fence, I sighed: "Thank you, Lord, thank you for taking care of me today. Thank you for what you are going to do for me tomorrow. For whatever comes into my life, I thank you."

I had no idea he was going to answer so quickly. Within a few days I was assigned a bed two nights a week in a shelter in Astoria, Queens.

As I signed in at the table, a young woman walked in from the kitchen. I looked up and my heart skipped a beat. There was my Dream Princess! I stared at her lustrous auburn hair. She had friendly eyes and there was a glow about her face as she walked across the room. My hands trembled and I began composing a love song in my mind.

Haltingly I struck up a conversation. Her name was Carol Ann Perkins. She was a volunteer worker in her mid-forties. She was polite and we talked a bit about my writing aspirations; then she left. But before she was out the door I had finished her song in my mind. A few days later I went to another shelter, at the Community United Methodist Church in Jackson Heights, where I had come to know the pastor, the Reverend Austin H. Armitstead. He gave me a typewriter and I typed out the song about my Dream Princess.

Meeting Carol Ann sparked a positive change in my life. I found a part-time job refereeing high school and college athletic events. My self-confidence grew.

Three weeks after meeting Carol Ann, I was again a guest at the shelter where she was a volunteer. Having saved a little money, I asked her out to lunch. For a moment I was afraid she was going to turn me down. Then, smiling, she hesitantly said yes. We went to a Roy Rogers and over hamburgers fell into easy conversation. I could see there was hurt in her eyes, and I cautiously drew her out. She said she had just ended a relationship with someone and then quickly changed the subject. We parted as friends, but that was all.

Even so, I excitedly phoned my mother about finding my Dream Princess. She said she would pray for her. I asked Carol Ann out again, and this time I brought her a single red rose. For the next four months our relationship continued over lunches, but always on a casual, friendly basis, and obviously not going anywhere. I, of course, was head over heels in love but didn't want to push myself.

"Oh, Father," I prayed, "this is the girl you showed me in my dream, but she doesn't seem interested in me at all. What should I do?" It turned out I didn't have to do anything. A few days later I discovered a new Carol Ann. I sensed a special warmth in her green eyes, and when she placed her hand on mine as we talked, I was ecstatic.

Later I learned that a friend of hers was making a pilgrimage to the Shrine of Our Lady of Guadalupe in Mexico. Carol Ann had given her a prayer petition to take, asking for "someone who is kind and gentle, good and loving and only has eyes for me." It was then she realized that the one courting her was all of those things.

On February 12, 1992, I got down on one knee and with a red rose in hand asked Carol Ann to marry me. Our wedding was officiated by pastor

Armitstead and Bishop Douglas L. Trees. A friend, Frank Scafuri, sang "Dreamer, I Wanna Be With You," the song he and I composed from the words I wrote after I first saw Carol Ann.

Since then we have made beautiful music together, and every week my Dream Princess still receives a single red rose from me. Carol Ann and I are both working and we volunteer at the two church shelters where I once slept.

Every so often someone down and out looks at me with pain-filled eyes and asks, "How can you possibly understand what I'm going through?" I sit down with him, put my arm around his shoulders and explain I know exactly what he's going through. I tell him God gives each of us a dream. And if we follow his will, pray and hold on to our faith even through the darkest times, our dreams will come true. Then I tell him about Carol Ann.

Published on Guideposts (https://www.guideposts.org).

Used with permission

Just Joey Rose photographed by Jean Harkin

VISITING GRANDMA by Jean Harkin

My grandmother is expecting twins! Yes, it is quite a shock. Though Grandma is a funny lady, especially when her deaf ear mishears and misinterprets what is said, she is also wise and down-to-earth. It can't be true that she is pregnant. How in the world at eighty-one!

I could hardly wait to find out the true story when I returned home from college for the summer. On my first visit to Grandma in the nursing home, I was told that she had changed a lot since my mother *dumped her* there. Grandma had arrived as her sprightly self but soon changed into a dreamy, out-of-touch person. *Were they giving her drugs to tone down her liveliness?*

* * *

As I enter her room (shocking in its cramped size compared to the spacious apartment where I'd last seen her) I sniff her talcum-powder scent but can't see her in the dim light. Then I realize she is the blanketed lump on the bed.

I walk over. Tapping her with my hand, "Hi Grandma—it's me!" The lump jerks, and out from under a brown blanket pokes a little wrinkled face— like a burrowing animal. "Hi Grandma!" I repeat.

She sits up, and her eyes sparkle. "I knew you'd come!" We embrace. "I have so much to tell you!" she says.

I'm looking forward to sharing our usual *girl time*—her gossip about friends and family, my college doings and boyfriends. Before I can say anything, she starts, "You know I'm having twins—a boy and a girl—any day now. That's why I'm here." Gulp! How to respond?

A nurse walks in with a pitcher of ice water and fills Grandma's bedside glass. She shoots a look at me. "Grandma's having twins," I say.

"Yes, among other things." The nurse smiles and pats Grandma on one hand.

I go with Grandma's story and ask her, "So have you picked out names yet?"

"Names for what?"

"The twins."

"What twins?" She looks around. "Do you like this compartment?" Her upper arms hang like a cape as she makes a sweeping motion at the room. "It's the largest one on the train. They think I'm royalty." She giggles.

"Where are you going?"

135

"To Egypt, I think."

Time to return to reality. "I'm just back from college in Nebraska, Grandma."

"I'm so glad you could catch this train!"

"Do you like it here okay?"

"Yes. I'm having the time of my life," Grandma responds. "Sometimes I've believed as many as six impossible things before breakfast." I remember that line from when I was a child, snuggling with Grandma in her cozy pink-cushioned rocking chair. Grandma and I went *Through the Looking-Glass* with *Alice* many times.

I sit down beside her on the bed and cuddle up. "So what now?"

She stares, seeming not to understand.

"What adventures are you looking forward to, Grandma?"

"Oh—let me tell you…" Her brown eyes twinkle, and she is the grandmother I've always known and loved.

Soul Mates photographed by Micah Harkin